Penology

SAGE COURSE COMPANIONS

KNOWLEDGE AND SKILLS *for* SUCCESS

Penology

David Scott

Los Angeles | London | New Delhi
Singapore | Washington DC

First published 2008
Reprinted 2013

SAGE Publications Ltd
1 Oliver's Yard
55 City Road
London EC1Y 1SP

SAGE Publications Inc
2455 Teller Road
Thousand Oaks, California 91320

SAGE Publications India Pvt Ltd
B 1/I 1 Mohan Cooperative Industrial Area
Mathura Road,
New Delhi 110 044

SAGE Publications Asia-Pacific Pte Ltd
3 Church Street
#10-04 Samsung Hub
Singapore 049483

Library of Congress Control Number: 2007932778

British Library Cataloguing in Publication data

A catalogue record for this book is available from the British Library

ISBN 978-1-4129-4810-4
ISBN 978-1-4129-4811-1 (pdk)

Typeset by C&M Digitals (P) Ltd., Chennai, India
Printed in Great Britain by the MPG Books Group
Printed on paper from sustainable resources

contents

part one
penology

Core area: **1.1 thinking like a penologist**

1.1

thinking like a penologist: an introduction to your course companion

Core areas: **introduction to the series**
how to use this book
structure of the book and key features
fugitive thought: a brief introduction to penology
thinking like a penologist

Introduction to the series

Welcome to the *Sage Course Companion: Penology*. Many people are drawn to the study of punishments, crime control and other means of responding to wrongdoing and social deviance. Those who harm, and how we should best respond to those harms, fascinate us. This focus on punishment and penal institutions, such as the prison, and their possible justifications is the remit of what is called 'penology'. Students can approach penological subject matter from various different academic disciplines, such as history, social policy, or the social sciences. The study of penology is a fast-growing area in many universities and, while there are many specialist books and introductory textbooks, it is difficult for those who are new to the subject to work out what best to read and in what order. The intention of this book is to provide you with a one-stop, easy-to-use reference guide that covers the main themes of prison and punishment modules.

The book is not intended to act as a replacement for lectures, textbooks, journal articles or specialist contributions in the field, but rather as a complement to such materials. In short, the aim of this book is to help you to get the most from your studies. If this text can either clarify and make sense of a complex penological debate, stimulate your interest, encourage you to look at issues in more depth, or help you use your imagination to start thinking more creatively about how social problems can be conceived of or addressed, then it will have achieved its aim—and perhaps much more.

How to use this book

This book is specifically designed to help undergraduate and postgraduate students on prison and punishment modules to succeed. This includes students on a range of degree programmes, including those studying law, humanities, anthropology, sociology, psychology, philosophy, health studies, political sciences, business management, and criminology and criminal justice. The book introduces some of the common principles and concepts of the discipline; it provides hints, tips and handy summaries of the main themes and issues; and, ultimately, it aims to enhance your understanding of, and ability to use, penological knowledge. For undergraduate students, this book can act as a revision guide and can help with passing exams. It should help you to structure and organise your thoughts, and it should enable you to get the most from your textbooks and the other reading that you do as part of your course. The book is also a helpful starting point for students doing a dissertation or postgraduate research project in penology, especially those who have not previously undertaken a penology module. I also hope that the book appeals to the general reader who is looking for a straightforward introduction to, and summary of, penology that is easily digestible and can be read relatively quickly. Overall, the course companion should help you to challenge common-sense and populist assumptions about 'crime' and punishment, and help you to think critically about the subject matter.

Course companions are designed to point you in the direction of key thinkers and key ideas, and to give you the briefest of introductions to their work and how to put their work in context. This, of course, is only a starting point, which must be followed up with wider reading and reflection. You should use your companion to supplement, not to replace, other sources, such as recommended course textbooks. In addition, you must continue to follow the course you have undertaken. Familiarise yourself with lecture content and seminar questions, because these will give you the best guide to what your examiner will be looking for in your exams and coursework. Look carefully at your penology module booklets, and at the readings and themes that they highlight. Unless you are a general reader, you need only focus on the themes that are identified by the module or course you are studying. Look to the chapters that reflect the course and what is most relevant to you at this given moment. Finally, the key to success at undergraduate and postgraduate level is wider reading. When you have finished a chapter, go to the actual sources and texts cited here and read them for yourselves. This is the best and most enjoyable way of studying.

Structure of the book and key features

The book is divided into four main parts. Part one provides you with an introduction to your course companion and explains how you can make the most of using this book. You are given a brief introduction to the discipline, followed by guidance on how you can learn to think like a penologist. Here, you are given advice on how to enter the mindset of penal experts and you are introduced to the kind of terminology that they use.

Part two starts by identifying the 'running themes' in penology that recur throughout the core curriculum, which is then overviewed in the following 11 chapters. These begin with a discussion of the philosophical and sociological accounts of punishment and imprisonment, and then move on to identify some of the key sources of penal knowledge. The book is largely focused on prisons and punishment in the United Kingdom, but the next chapter in part two examines international comparative studies of penology and their implications for thinking about penal sanctions closer to home. The next three chapters provide an account of the history, aims, policy and organisational structures of penal systems in the United Kingdom, before moving on to consider some of the problems and controversies that are encountered in prison life and the current means of penal accountability. Part two concludes with a discussion of non-custodial forms of punishment and a review of three alternative visions of the future: penal expansionism; penal reductionism; and penal abolitionism. Many, if not all, of these issues will be discussed in your course, but you must ensure that you are clear regarding the focus and content of the module you are studying. This can only be achieved by attending lectures and seminars. Reading appropriate chapters in advance, however, may help you to understand your lectures and to prepare for your seminars.

To help you in your studies, the book provides bullet points of key arguments and debates throughout. Alongside this, your course companion uses the following unique features to help you to develop insights into penological thought.

- **Running themes** Each chapter starts with a list of central themes in penology. All of the running themes are listed together at the start of part two.
- **Key penologists** At the start of many chapters, three important penologists are highlighted, each of whom has made very significant contributions to the area under discussion.
- **Summary boxes** These boxes highlight and summarise some of the key issues on a given topic.
- **Tips** and **common pitfalls** Tips boxes appear throughout the chapters and offer you key factors to remember, along with advice on what to do and how to best answer a question; common pitfalls remind you of common mistakes and give you some indication of what not to do. These boxes will also help you to question dominant assumptions and common-sense ideas on 'crime' and punishment.
- **Questions** At the end of every chapter in part two and dispersed throughout part three, you are given example questions and indications of how these might be answered.
- **Taking it further** At the end of every chapter in part two, you are given details of recent debates, penal controversies or examples of in-depth readings on that topic area.
- **Textbook guide** These guides offer you a list of some of the best books to read first when developing your knowledge in a module or to undertake as background reading for a dissertation.

Part three offers you guidance with your studies. This should be read in conjunction with part two. If you work your way carefully through part three, by its end, you should be better equipped to profit from your lectures, benefit from your seminars, construct your essays efficiently, develop effective revision strategies and respond comprehensively to the pressures of exam situations and, finally, think clearly about the organisation and structure of your dissertation. In the five chapters in this part, you are presented with checklists and bullet points to focus your attention on key issues; worked examples to demonstrate the use of such features as structure, headings and continuity; and tips that provide practical advice in nutshell form.

Part four concludes the book with a glossary that provides brief definitions of a number of key penological terms and a bibliography listing the sources cited in the book.

Fugitive thought: a brief introduction to penology

We all have been punished and have probably perpetrated some form of punishment at some stage of our lives. Although the discipline of penology has been primarily concerned with punishments sanctioned and undertaken by the state, it is important to recognise that punishment does not begin there, but rather within wider society. Punishments can be physical or psychological, performed publicly or privately, and can be either informal or a formal and legal sanction. You may have experienced some form of sanction or punishment by a family member while as a child at home, or at school through informal interactions with friends or for breaking school rules. As an adult, such informal punishments may take place in relationships or in the workplace. You may feel that this form of punishment has served you well in your life, or you may have found it no use at all. From this experience, you may think that punishment is a 'necessary evil'—that is essential for the raising of children or for the regulation of adult human life—or it may have led you to think that such sanctioning is counterproductive.

Punishments are invoked when someone is believed to have done something wrong. This means that they are believed to have breached the rules, whether those rules are legal, social, organisational or moral. Wrongdoing and rule breaking are probably inevitable in human societies, and so the pertinent question becomes 'how should we respond when wrongful acts and breaches of rules occur?' Should we aim to include or exclude offenders, to help them, to control them, or to harm them? Alongside this, we must also recognise that the manner in which rules are defined and understood may vary over time and space. Rule breaking and doing wrong reflect the different interests, values and goals of those in positions of power, and of those who define the rules in the first instance. Consequently, some wrongdoing is illegal and defined as a 'crime', while other forms of harm are not. Further, whether a person is punished for a wrongdoing is not only a consequence of the act itself. It is just as important to think about who the offender is. You may often have heard the term 'don't do as I do, do as I say': an adult or teacher (people in positions of power in a given social context) who breaches family or school rules may be much less likely to face sanctions than a child or student (the powerless) who does the same.

The nature and extent of action that the government and its official servants take in response to human wrongdoing tells us a great deal about the kind of society in which we live. Many penologists and politicians have highlighted over the centuries that the way in which we deal with offenders is a major indication of the level of civilisation and commitment to human rights and civil liberties in our society. The study of punishment and penalties, then, is not only about those who are subjected to them, or even those who work in the criminal justice system, but is something that goes to the heart of our culture. We may only be bystanders in the punishment business, but it is in our names—and apparently our interests—that the harms of punishment are inflicted.

The study of punishment has a very long history. There are documents detailing penal philosophy in the times of the great Greek civilisation, and both Plato and Aristotle wrote on punishment. There is also evidence of penal theory in the Egyptian and Roman civilisations. You have probably heard the saying 'an eye for an eye, a tooth for a tooth'. This phrase is derived from the ancient Jewish tradition of lex talionis. Although it is still widely used today, its real meaning of restoring balance is often misinterpreted. The great social thinkers, sociologists and philosophers—from Kant and Hegel, to Durkheim and Foucault—have all written about punishment, with the latter writing also on imprisonment. But the discipline of penology is often seen as emerging in the eighteenth century, with the philosophical insights of Cesare Beccaria and Jeremy Bentham, alongside the penal reforms inspired by evangelical Christians such as John Howard and George Onesiphourus Paul. What all of this indicates is that the history of 'fugitive thought' is closely tied up with a number of different disciplines, and with the work of penal practitioners and reformers. You should be aware that this multidisciplinary approach and pragmatic application of knowledge continues to shape the discipline of penology today.

What is penology?

Penology is a multidisciplinary subject that aims to study and evaluate the application of penal sanctions to wrongdoers. It has broadly focused on the justifications, characteristics and effectiveness of penal institutions. Since the eighteenth century, many penologists have conceived of prison as a place with rehabilitative potential, emphasising its role as a means of reducing reoffending or of instilling moral backbone into offenders. More recently, penologists have expanded their remit to examine the daily lives and culture of prisoners and staff, and some of the inherent dangers of confinement. Since the 1960s, penologists who are very critical of the penal system have evaluated its practices and legitimacy, calling for society to end the use of imprisonment and to consider non-punitive responses to wrongdoing and rule breaking.

Penology attempts to understand the complex, difficult and emotive issues that are raised when we think about punishment.

✓ Penologists are interested in the responses to human wrongdoing and, specifically, in the practices, forms and evolution of the punishment and social controls that exist in contemporary society.

✓ Penologists focus on the criminal justice system and develop arguments concerning its legitimacy.

✓ Although united in their focus of investigation, penologists come from a wide range of disciplines, including psychology, geography, history, philosophy, social policy, sociology and criminology.

✓ In general, penologists look to understand the deployment of penalties within their social, historical, economic and political contexts.

✓ When thinking about the criminal justice system, penologists use their 'imagination' and do not take the practices, or even existence, of punishment at a straightforward or common-sense level.

✓ Unlike practitioners, who are concerned almost exclusively with the operational practices, laws and procedures shaping punishments and their apparent effectiveness, penologists also ask broader questions concerning who we punish, for what offence, when and why.

✓ Penologists are interested in the justifications of penalties and social sanctions, and develop a specific theoretical framework that informs, and shapes, their research and arguments.

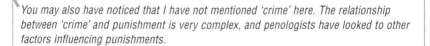

You may also have noticed that I have not mentioned 'crime' here. The relationship between 'crime' and punishment is very complex, and penologists have looked to other factors influencing punishments.

Thinking like a penologist

The key to success in your course is to learn how to 'think like a penologist'—that is to say, to learn how to speak *academic* language, using the terms and phrases that mark out 'penologist speak' from that of everyday talk on 'crime', punishment and imprisonment. This book will give you hints and tips about when and how to use this language, and on the ways of thinking about the world that come with this language. It is important that you use the appropriate terms and phrases— but there are no easy shortcuts here: you must be able to unpack terms and use them. Academic language is a form of shorthand and, to get good marks, you must be able to demonstrate that you fully understand the words you are using, and their implications for the deployment of penalties in society.

To think like a penologist it is important that you think critically about prisons and punishment. This does not mean that you simply criticise everyone and everything, but rather that you are able to develop analytical skills that help you to evaluate and judge the issues that you are studying. 'Crime' and punishment are popular debates, but discussions are often rooted in complete misunderstandings of key facts and issues. The kind of stories and debates that you hear generally, in pub talk or on a radio phone-in, are pragmatic, individualistic and authoritarian. You must allow yourself the opportunity to think beyond such penological illiteracy. You must be able to develop an analytical and critical framework when assessing the validity and appropriateness of current forms of punishment and imprisonment, and to engage with wider social theory, philosophy, social policy, history, psychology and, especially, sociology.

Thinking like a penologist involves challenging taken-for-granted and populist assumptions. It involves taking on what appears, at first, to be quite alien ideas. One of the most remarkable arguments made by penologists is that we should rethink the relationship between 'crime' and punishment. You have probably grown up and lived your life with the belief that the existence of punishments is intimately tied to the problem of 'crime', and that the extent of 'crime' is the most important factor in determining the level of punishment. But some of the most important and influential penologists, such as Emile Durkheim, Georg Rusche and Michel Foucault, argue that 'crime' is relatively insignificant, and that the form and extent of punishments in society must be understood through its relationship with other social, economic and political factors. Thinking like a penologist means *thinking outside the box.*

Some penologists put the word 'crime' in inverted commas to indicate that the content and meanings of the term are contested. They may offer alternative words, such as 'troubles', 'problematic behaviours' or 'social harms' to describe rule breaking and wrongdoing.

Penology is a theoretical discipline and, when theorising about punishment and imprisonment, it is important that you are able to locate the issues and debates within the 'big picture'. One of the best ways to do this is to develop what has been described as your *'sociological* or *criminological imagination'* (Mills, 1959; Barton et al., 2006). This is a quality of mind, a particular way of approaching, thinking about or interpreting social problems and their possible implications and resolution. Unlike 'pub talk', you look to uncover wider social, political and economic factors that might influence who is punished and why. Central to penological thought are concerns around power. This entails analysis of the form and nature of wider power relations in society, and of the exercise of the power to punish. You must constantly be aware of 'power' when thinking about punishment: who has the power to define and label; who are the powerless; who are the powerful; and how these power differentials shape crime controls.

To think like a penologist, you should attempt to understand punishments within their structural, historical and social contexts. You should try to form an understanding of the world in which individual choices, experiences and daily lives are located within a given historical moment and wider structural contexts, such as age, gender, sexuality, financial resources or perceived 'race'. You should consider how the wrongdoing and rule breaking of people at the lower end of the social hierarchy may be perceived and treated differently to that of those at the top. You should also try to see things from different perspectives and points of view, including the world views of the prisoner and the powerless.

Using your imagination

It is perhaps stating the obvious to say that the only people who can tell us what the experience of imprisonment is really like are those who have actually been in prison. You can, however, study penological and sociological research on prison culture, and/or read prisoner autobiographies to gain some insight of what it would be like to be imprisoned. What is clear from these sources is that prison is a lonely, isolating, disempowering, brutalising and dehumanising experience.

Imagine being locked in your bathroom—put an inspection hole in the door; put bars on the windows; remove the bath and, in its place, put three beds. Then imagine what it might be like to spend 15–23 hours a day in this 'cell'. Imagine what it would be like if the two people you most dislike in the world were to be in the cell with you. You must eat, sleep and 'shit' in your cell in the company of others, and it is possible that all three activities may be going on in this small space at the same time. If you leave your

---

(Continued)

'bathroom/cell', you have only very limited choices, power or sense of personal responsibility: somebody else will open doors for you; somebody else will tell you what to do, where to go, when to eat, work, sleep and, perhaps, even when to speak.

This may be a worst-case scenario in relation to imprisonment in many Western nations, but it remains an all-too-common reality of prison life in the United Kingdom in 2008. Using our imaginations in this way presents us with a frightening picture of the potential impact of imprisonment on the conception of the self, even before we start to talk about the minuets of prison life: the (poor) quality of the food; the limited access to family friends, and constructive activities; the negative attitudes and treatment of other prisoners or of the staff guarding you. It is difficult to see how this environment can do anything to help the perpetrator to acknowledge the harmfulness of their wrongful behaviour or meet the needs of the victim of the harm, except perhaps to satisfy their understandable, although not necessarily healthy, retributive emotions or to provide a symbolic reaction denouncing the problematic event. Yet prison persists. Its costs are varied. But all are very high.

When thinking like a penologist you can develop a new vocabulary for understanding the lived experiences of those you are studying. Using your sociological imagination as Charles Wright Mills (1959) intended can help you to develop ways of understanding the social world that intimately connect individual meanings and experiences with wider collective or social realities. Moreover, it should help you to understand why many penologists believe that prisons must be placed within wider social and structural contexts, rather than considered in isolation. To 'think like a penologist', then, means to develop such an imagination when contemplating punishments.

part two

core areas of the curriculum

Core areas: **running themes in penology**

2.1 justifications of punishment

2.2 theorising about prisons and punishment

2.3 sources of penal knowledge

2.4 comparative penologies

2.5 the history and aims of imprisonment

2.6 penal policy

2.7 penal administration and prisoner populations

2.8 sociologies of prison life

2.9 penal accountability

2.10 probation and community penalties

2.11 future directions and alternative visions

running themes in penology

No matter what area of penology you are writing about, it is probably not too difficult to predict that the subject in question will be marked out by similar 'running themes' that recur throughout the subject.

Always try to mention these themes and to think about how they make an impact upon the topic at hand.

- **Alternatives to prison** Non-custodial ways of dealing with wrongdoing. These can involve community penalties and other ways of dealing with harms and wrongs that do not adopt the punitive rationale.
- **Human rights** A normative principle that is based on the recognition of the innate dignity of a fellow human being. This can involve the recognition of legal entitlements and of the wrongdoer's shared humanity, and acknowledgement of all human suffering.
- **Labour market** The thesis that there are strong links between the form and nature of punishment, and the needs of the labour market.
- **Legitimacy** The moral and political validity of the exercise of penal power. The criteria defining what a legitimate response to wrongdoing entails are hotly contested and there are a number of different approaches to thinking about penal legitimacy. These include theories from Emile Durkheim (on ritualism and the lack of legitimacy), Max Weber (on the belief in legitimacy and authority), David Beetham (on how institutions must conform to people's beliefs), and Gramscian and (neo-)abolitionist perspectives that call for philosophical and normative criteria for evaluating the rightfulness of punishments.
- **Less eligibility** The belief that conditions of imprisonment must not be higher than the living conditions of the poorest labourer. Adoption of this doctrine has major implications for the dehumanisation of wrongdoers.
- **Managerialism** A credo that claims that better forms of management, rooted in the principles of efficiency, effectiveness and economy, can solve the current penal crisis and provide services that are better value for money. It is an ethos that has dominated public services in the United Kingdom in the last twenty years.
- **Pains of imprisonment** The inherent deprivations of prison life, as coined by Gresham Sykes (1958), who described the '*pains of imprisonment*' for male prisoners as the deprivation of liberty, of heterosexual sex, of goods and services, of autonomy and of security.
- **Penal reform** The argument that the prison can be improved and made more humane or effective. Penal reformers are often humanitarians who believe

that prisons can rehabilitate, if used for the appropriate people, and can have good living conditions.

- **Power to punish** The definition and application of the penal rationale to discipline, exclude or control human behaviour. Penal critics have highlighted how the power to punish is disproportionately deployed against the poor and powerless.
- **Public protection** The claim that prison and community penalties exist to contain dangerous offenders and those people who pose a considerable threat to ordinary members of society. Public protection is a major justification for increasing levels of prison security.
- **Rehabilitation** A justification of punishment, which claims that prison can be used to restore an offender to his or her previous competency. The term is now often used interchangeably with 'reform'.
- **Risk** A highly influential way of calculating and assessing the danger or harm that an offender may present in the future.
- **Social divisions** Who loses and who gains in a given social context. Penologists have paid particular attention to examining divisions centred on poverty, social exclusion, 'race', gender and age.
- **Social justice** The equitable redistribution of the social product, allowing individuals to meet their necessary needs. Alongside this, it requires a rebalancing of power, a reducing of vulnerabilities, and the fostering of trust, security and social inclusion. It also implies recognition and respect for the shared humanity of wrongdoers, whoever they may be.

Remember!

It is a good bet that, whatever you are writing about, most of these running themes can be squeezed into your essay or exam to give you a more rounded and wide-ranging answer.

Bear in mind that the running themes listed above are nearly always interrelated.

2.1

justifications of punishment

Core areas: **the five rules of punishment**
punishing future crimes
punishing past crimes
thinking beyond punishment

Running themes

- Alternatives to prison
- Human rights
- Legitimacy
- Penal reform
- Public protection
- Rehabilitation
- Risk
- Social divisions

Key penologists

Cesar Beccaria (1738–94) Considered by many scholars to be the most influential Enlightenment thinker on penal reform in Europe, Beccaria was born to Milanese nobility and studied law at the University of Pavia, Italy. Under the guidance of his friend Alessandro Verri, Beccaria published his most significant treatise *Essays on Crimes and Punishment* in 1764. This has become one of the foundational texts in penology and was hugely influential, in terms of both the theories of punishment and the development of modern criminal justice systems in Europe, the USA and beyond. Beccaria promoted the ideas that punishments should be justified through deterrence, and that sanctions must be certain and proportionate to the offence committed.

Jeremy Bentham (1748–1832) A philosopher and lawyer who had a massive influence on theories of punishment and the design of the penitentiary. He was awarded a law degree from Oxford, but moved away from legal reforms towards advocating the wider philosophical credo of utilitarianism, which promoted the '*greatest happiness of the greatest number*'. He is famous for his 'panopticon' prison design, which, although never built, influenced Victorian prison architecture in the United Kingdom and prisons in the USA, such as Stateville. Although he constantly petitioned the British government to run a panopticon prison for profit in England, he never succeeded in this goal. When he died, Bentham had his body stuffed and it still can be seen on display.

Thomas Mathiesen (born 1933) A highly influential contemporary Norwegian penologist. Thomas Mathiesen is Professor of Sociology of Law at the University of Oslo. Mathiesen co-founded the Norwegian prisoner union KROM in 1968, and his Marxist studies and penal activism led him to advocate penal abolitionism. His key books include *The Politics of Abolition* (1974), which has had massive influence on the radical prison lobby in the United Kingdom, and *Prison On Trial*, originally published in 1990 and in its third edition (2006), which is one of the most impressive critical overviews of the philosophy of punishment ever written.

The five rules of punishment

Penologists have asked important philosophical questions about all forms of punishment, regulation and control. We are to consider the following three:

- what is state punishment?
- are state punishments necessary and justifiable?
- do we need to punish at all?

Let us start by thinking about the first question: 'What is state punishment?' Broadly speaking, a 'punishment' is an act that intentionally inflicts pain on another person. Punishment is about deliberately causing somebody else harm and suffering, perhaps in response to an illegal act. It also implies that somebody has the right or the legitimate power to create human suffering. The most influential definition of punishment has been provided by Professor Andrew Flew (1954), who argued that, for an act to be defined as a punishment, it must conform to five basic rules.

The five rules of punishment

The penal sanction must:

1. create human suffering;
2. arise as a direct result of the perpetration of an offence;
3. only be directed at the person who undertook the offence, i.e. the offender;
4. be the intentional creation of other humans in response to that offence;
5. be inflicted by an authorised body representing the embodiment of the rules or laws of the society in which the offence was committed.

For a given penal sanction to be understood as a *state punishment*, it must arise through a person's illegal wrongdoing, it must be painful to the offender and it must be imposed only by state officials who have been given the power to punish in that given society. Following this reasoning, any suffering that is meted out in response to a 'crime' by non-authorised personnel, i.e. vigilantes, must be condemned as illegitimate.

But the very idea of organised practices that are rooted in the deliberate infliction of human pain and suffering necessarily raises key moral and political questions of 'legitimacy'. This leads us to our second question: 'Are state punishments necessary and justifiable?'

Justifications of punishment can be divided into three main approaches: philosophies that look to justify punishment in terms of preventing future offending behaviour; philosophies that focus on responding to the actual offence; and philosophies that maintain that punishment can be neither morally nor politically justified.

Main philosophical approaches to the justification of punishment

Future crimes

- Reform and rehabilitation
- Individual and general deterrence
- Prevention, protection and incapacitation

(Continued)

Past crimes

- **Retribution, denunciation and just deserts**

Beyond punishment

- **Redress**
- **Reparation, restitution and restorative justice**

Punishing future crimes

Reform and rehabilitation

The terms 'reform' and 'rehabilitation', although often used interchangeably, in fact mean very different things. Reform ultimately means the changing of the offender. The aim of reformative punishment is to alter the individual by attempting to re-educate, teach, train or instil a new morality. The transformation of the offender would have been necessary even if he or she had not committed the particular act for which he or she is currently incarcerated, because the offender's immorality, irresponsibility or lack of respectability is rooted in either cultural deprivation or individual weakness. The offender is in need of moral education, in the form of work, religion, schooling or vocational training.

Rehabilitation, by contrast, does not attempt to change the offender, but rather to restore the individual to that state in which he or she was before the crime was committed. It is assumed that the individual has, in some way, been changed through the 'crime' he or she has committed, or that the 'crime' occurred because of the offender's mental, physical or moral degradation. This suggests that treatment is most important and that, just like medicine, if the problems could be correctly diagnosed, we would be able to cure the offender and, ultimately, society of problematic behaviour. This idea is linked to the medical model, and the importance of forensic psychology, psychiatry, and medical experts.

Common pitfall *Be careful, when an essay or exam question asks about 'reform', not to confuse the philosophical justification about individual change with ideas about changes in the system, such as improving prison environments, or the introduction of new laws and penal sanctions.*

In practice, rehabilitation and reform have been applied together. Perhaps most well known was the 'treatment and training ideology' that provided the orientating focus of the prison service in the United Kingdom in the mid-twentieth century. Underscoring both reform and rehabilitation are the beliefs that:

- offenders are different to 'normal' people and that this difference is directly linked to their offending behaviour;
- we can positively alter or 'normalise' people through social engineering and that we have the right to do so;
- punishment, generally, and imprisonment, specifically, can act as a catalyst for this restoration or alteration of the offender.

According to Philip Bean (1981), the key strengths to the rehabilitation argument are that:

- it treats people as individuals and attempts to deal with the actual person and context of the crime;
- it promotes individual responsibilities;
- it places emphasis on the personal lives of the offenders, focusing on offender motivations and possible processes that can be invoked to challenge offending or to help someone to cope with life;
- it allows for flexibility and new ways of responding to offending behaviour, such as developing constructive sentences. In this sense, something good comes from the 'evil of punishment'.

But reform and rehabilitation have been heavily criticised.

1 'Crime' is not an illness or disease, but a social construct. It may be a perfectly understandable response to a specific set of circumstances. Offenders may not necessarily be different from other people, and their behaviour may reflect the labelling process that is imposed by those with the power to define.

2 We are moral beings who must be allowed to make choices. Humans should not be treated like animals, to be conditioned or trained.

3 Many alleged cures do not actually work and treatments can create more harm than that of the initial wrong.

4 The sentence is open-ended, thus undermining due process. The offender must complete the proposed transformation, or be cured, before release.

Do prisons rehabilitate or dehabilitate offenders?

After nearly two hundred years of the prison experiment in the United Kingdom, it seems that a sentence of imprisonment is more likely to increase, rather than to decrease, future offending.

1 The prison environment is dehumanising and dehabilitating. The inherent pains of imprisonment are likely to be counterproductive. Further, the act of imprisonment may lead to the embedding of a psychology that promotes the rejection of rejecters, therefore building barriers to positive learning.

2 The prison is a 'school for scoundrels'. Prisons are universities of 'crime' and prisoners can learn new skills from their peers.

3 Can we learn how to live when we are free while we are in captivity? People act differently in prison to how they do on the outside. Incarceration may even lead to people losing skills that are essential for coping on the outside. The harms of imprisonment are also likely to exacerbate any social or psychological problems that the prisoner may have had before coming to prison.

***

Common pitfall   *Ensure that, when looking at a question on punishment, you are clear on whether you are being asked to evaluate the philosophical justifications or how effective they have been when used in prison. It is possible that the question will be asking you to assess both the philosophy and its practical application.*

***

Individual and general deterrence

The philosophical justifications concerning deterrence are rooted in utilitarianism, a moral and political philosophy that emphasises the importance of developing social policies that maximise the good and minimise the bad. Utilitarians believe that we are able to devise an equation between pain and pleasure. In relation to punishment, this relates specifically to the pains of punishment as a utility in reducing the pains inflicted upon victims. Utilitarians argue that we can work out a system of punishment that can discourage and deter offending behaviour. This means that the system must be certain and that 'crimes' must be punished.

There are two central issues concerning deterrence: individual and general. Individual deterrence involves the punishments having a direct impact on the offender who has committed the offence. This is clearly a psychological approach. General deterrence is applied to the whole community, i.e. as a method of social control.

Individual deterrence

For Bean (1981), individual deterrence is directly linked to the following.

1. **Physical freedoms** To break the law in wider society, we must be empowered in various ways. Individual deterrence is rooted in the power of an institution to prevent the offender physically from committing an offence in public spaces.

2. **Conditioning** The punishment is intended to remove the desire to offend from the offender by bringing about a psychological change in that offender.

3. **Individual fear calculus** The desire to offend is kept in check by the fear of the consequences should the person be caught. The rationality of the offender is emphasised in this approach, with the offender deciding that the pleasure of crime cannot outweigh the pain of imprisonment.

General deterrence

General deterrence involves social control and central to this is the 'social fear calculus'. It works in a similar way to the individual fear calculus, but the individual is not subjected to the pain him or herself; rather, the individual sees the pain of others and is deterred from the activity that led to it, because he or she does not want to be subjected to such suffering. It relates to wider social relations and, although directed against an individual, is intended to have implications beyond the person who is actually punished.

Deterring who? The limitations of deterrence

There are a number of problems with the deterrent approach, as follows.

1. Can we scientifically measure pain and pleasure? Is it possible to quantify the individual human experiences of pain and pleasure, and to devise a calculus that can produce an equation of equivalence? Can we actually compare the pain of being a victim of crime to that of a punishment?

2 Can we scientifically measure the deterrent effect? On both the social and individual levels, we do not know if deterrence actually works. 'Recidivism' normally measures the reconviction of offenders within two years of release. Recidivism rates are high for both young (75 per cent) and adult (50 per cent) offenders. This will always be an underestimate, because the figures do not include those who reoffend and are not caught.

3 How can we be certain that others will react to these deterrents in the same way in which you or I would? What may deter me may not deter you, and vice versa.

4 Do we all sit down and calculate the consequences of our every action? What about impulsive and opportunistic 'crime'? Much wrongdoing, including serious harms, does not necessarily rely upon rational choice.

5 Harsh sentences do not work. There is evidence of a correlation between harsh punishments and a decrease in recorded drink-driving. What has not been proved, however, is whether this is a causal relationship. There has been a great deal of moral education on the dangers of drunk drivers and many people believe that you should either drink or drive. Evidence for other crimes would also suggest that there is not a particularly strong relationship between deterrence and crime reduction (Hudson, 2003).

> A **correlation** is when two phenomena occur at the same time, but are not necessarily linked. For example, a recorded increase in the consumption of carrot juice may coincide with a decline in recorded 'crime'. Both have happened at the same time, but are not linked with the other. The discovery of a **causal relationship** is the golden fleece of penology. A causal relationship is much more difficult to prove and arises only when one phenomenon has a direct relationship with another—in short, when there is a cause and effect.

6 Is it moral to punish a person so that it will deter others? Can we justify the infliction of pain onto one person in an attempt to deter others?

7 There is also a moral argument put forward stating that, if the aim of punishment is to deter the wider public, then it does not actually matter who is punished. The punished may be either guilty or innocent, but if it serves a wider utility and deters other people, the punishment is deemed to have been justified.

Prevention, protection and incapacitation

'Incapacitation' means the reduction of the capacity of the offender to commit crimes in order to protect the public. Right-wing extremists have called for the incapacitation of all criminals and there are many who consider arguments around selective incapacitation plausible. This justification has been attractive because it:

- can lead to the removal of persistent and dangerous offenders;
- reduces crime rates and state expenditure;
- has been a politically popular option.

The limitations of incapacitation

1 'Crime' is cyclical and generational, and, for incapacitation to work, we would have to constantly incarcerate large sections of each generation. The removal of (poor) persistent offenders only has an impact for a small number of years, after which their place is taken by a new, younger group of people.

2 Incapacitation is grounded in positivism, prediction and risk assessments. If we are to protect society, we must first be able to assess who is a risk to society. West and Farrington (1973) undertook to assess which of a group of seven-year-olds would be convicted of an offence by the age of 14 and which would still be offending at the age of 21. Remarkably, despite taking into account the normal indicators, they only got half of their assessments right. Such failure in prediction leads to *false negatives* or *false positives.*

False negatives and false positives

- False negatives offenders—on parole, for example—who have been regarded as unlikely to reoffend when released from prison. Predictions of low risk have been made, but the ex-offender has consequently reoffended.
- False positives Those who are wrongly predicted as being likely to reoffend. They are more difficult to discover, because they have been imprisoned. These people would not have offended had they been free.

Thomas Mathiesen (2006) asks us two very important questions in relation to false negatives and false positives.

1. Should we lock people up who have done nothing wrong?
2. If we make mistakes, should we lock people up who are not going to offend in order to protect ourselves from those who may reoffend in the future?

Despite the obvious limitations of positivism and prediction, there have been many studies, following in the tradition of West and Farrington (1973), that have been published by the government in recent years. You will be able to access these through the Home Office and the Ministry of Justice.

Punishing past crimes

Retribution, denunciation and just deserts

Talk of retribution is often linked with talk of 'justice'. The argument is that we get what we deserve. Retribution, in its various forms, is rooted in the principle that, if we harm another human being, we ourselves deserve to be harmed. The retributive approach to punishment has the advantage of focusing on an offender's guilt and thus equating the punishment to a wrong that has been done. It also argues for proportionality, in that lesser crimes should be punished in a lesser way and greater crimes, more harshly. Retributive punishments are a public statement that the behaviour punished is wrong and should not be engaged in. It shows that society disapproves of such behaviours. By punishing past crimes, we are demonstrating that the behaviour is wrong by denouncing them.

In recent times, retribution has been popularised through the arguments of 'just deserts'. This perspective has been championed in the work of Andrew von Hirsch (1976). In *Doing Justice*, von Hirsch argued that punishment should be commensurate to the seriousness of the offence. Just deserts, however, should not be seen as an all-encompassing justification for punishment; rather it is linked to sentencing and is called a 'distributive justification'. This means that it is involved in justifying the distribution or the meeting out of punishments. The difficulty that the idea of just deserts has encountered has centred on the measuring of the seriousness of a 'crime' and whether we should focus on the offender's *intentions* or the *consequences* of his or her wrongdoing.

Two wrongs? A critique of retribution

1. We live in an unequal society, in which the enforcement of the criminal law is focused upon working-class property offenders.

2. Thomas Mathiesen (2006) reminds us that the people we punish are generally poor, in terms both of finances and of life chances.

3 Braithwaite and Pettit (1990) point out that we only punish a small number of offenders. Is it right to continue with the punishment of the few, when the great majority of offenders never receive any formal punishment at all? Should we *scapegoat* the small minority or should we look to decrease our emphasis on punishment?

4 Is it healthy to want somebody else to experience pain and suffering? Does punishment further dehumanise offenders, leading to a greater likelihood of offending and dehumanise those who call for such human degradations?

5 Two wrongs cannot make a right: how can the infliction of more pain repair or redress the harm and pain created by the misdemeanour?

6 Perhaps the most significant philosophical failing of the retribution argument is that it fails to establish a case as to why someone should be punished in the first instance. We often hear the argument of an 'eye for an eye' or a 'life for a life', yet such principles were developed as a means of ensuring that, if a conflict existed between two Jewish tribes and lives were lost, the *lex talionis* was invoked to ensure that one tribe would not be destroyed. Contrary to current understandings, this did not mean that a life was taken for a life lost, but rather that a life was *given* from one tribe to another to ensure parity. The principle is not one of harm escalation or retribution, but one of the restoration of balance.

Common pitfall   *Ensure that you fully explore the meaning of all of the concepts that you use. Many terms have different meanings at different times to different people. Two obvious examples are 'justice' and 'lex talionis'.*

Ultimately, then, we are left with a number of serious problems and contradictions—and these concerns lead us to our third question: 'Do we need to punish at all?'

Thinking beyond punishment

Some penologists have challenged the legitimacy of punishment, and have looked beyond strategies of penalisation as means of responding to personal troubles, harms, social problems and illegalities. Abolitionist thinker Willem de Haan (1990) argues that we should think beyond punishment and offers the concept of 'redress' in its place. This is a concept with ancient origins and involves the consideration of historical and anthropological forms of dispute settlement and conflict resolution.

Redress means:

> to put right or in good order again, to remedy or remove trouble of any kind, to set right, to repair, rectify something suffered or complained of like a wrong to correct, amend, reform or do away with a bad or faulty state of things, to repair an action or misdeed or offence, to save or deliver from misery, to restore or bring back a person to a proper state, to happiness or prosperity, to the right course.

(*Concise Oxford Dictionary*, cited in de Haan, 1990, p. 158)

Similar principles are implied in the other 'R's of community responses: reparation; restitution; repayment; reconciliation; and reintegration. Stan Cohen (1985) reminds us that these are visions of inclusionary, rather than exclusionary, social control that are rooted in social integration and community. But informal means of control can lead to a further extension of state powers, and to new modes of discipline, surveillance and regulation. They can blur boundaries and may bring into the criminal justice system more petty offenders. They may also intensify state controls that are directed at serious offenders.

" Consider the moral and political arguments for and against incapacitation. "

Define and outline the main arguments of incapacitation. Then highlight the moral concerns: notably, that we do not have the ability to predict future behaviour and that there are consequently many who are punished even though they may not have reoffended. Move on to overview the political realities, pointing to the disproportionate control of people from poor and working-class backgrounds.

" Are the arguments for restorative justice plausible in a society with 'race', class and gender structural fault lines? "

First, explain the main principles of restorative justice, and then highlight how it does not address the fact that punishments are defined and shaped through wider social divisions. This inability to challenge power effectively leaves it vulnerable to be co-opted by the powerful—take, for example, the idea of restorative justice in prison. Finally, consider how this perspective leaves wider structural inequalities and injustices unchanged.

Taking it **FURTHER**

You have encountered a number of arguments that appear to indicate that it is actually very difficult to justify punishments for all people, at all times and in all different social circumstances. This goes against our common-sense assumptions that punishments continue to be used because, somehow, they work. Think critically about the following questions.

- Does punishment, overall, reduce or increase human pain?
- Does punishment repair the harm done in the wrongdoing?
- Does punishment reduce the recurrence of problematic incidents?
- Is the use of punishment morally justifiable?
- Why do we continue to punish people when it does not appear to work for human good?

Textbook guide

BEAN, P (1981) *Punishment: A Philosophical and Criminological Inquiry*, Oxford: Martin Robertson

CAVADINO, M AND DIGNAN, J (2007) *The Penal System*, 4th edn, London: Sage

GOLASH, D (2005) *The Case Against Punishment*, London: New York University Press

HONDERICH, T (2006) *Punishment: The Supposed Justifications Revisited*, London: Pluto Press

HUDSON, BA (2003) *Understanding Justice*, 2nd edn, Milton Keynes: Open University Press

MATHIESEN, T (2006) *Prison On Trial*, 3rd edn, Winchester: Waterside Press

2.2	
theorising about prisons and punishment	

Core areas: **progress, modernity and civilisation**

social divisions, power, and the distribution of punishments

 Running themes

- Labour market
- Legitimacy
- Less eligibility
- Penal reform
- Power to punish
- Risk
- Social divisions
- Social justice

Key penologists

Emile Durkheim (1858–1917) One of the founding fathers of sociology, Emile Durkheim is one of the most significant writers on the sociology of punishment. A French scholar who worked for many years at the Sorbonne in Paris, his main writings include PhD thesis *Division of Labour* (1893) and magnum opus *The Elementary Forms of Religious Life* (1912). Durkheim is often wrongly caricatured as a dry, conservative functionalist thinker who has little to offer, but he was, in fact, deeply radical for his time, making important contributions to moral philosophy. He was always a reformist socialist, rather than a revolutionary—but he was an idealist. He did not describe the functions of our society, but rather wanted to identify what society needed to resolve its conflicts and to develop a moral consensus. Durkheim's thought is an attempt to offer advice on how society could, or should, operate, rather than an assessment of how it currently is. Durkheim died, allegedly of a broken heart, not long after hearing that his son had been killed during the Great War.

Georg Rusche (1900–50) Rusche was a key Marxist thinker at the Frankfurt School, Germany, and co-wrote the foundational text of modern penology, *Punishment and Social Structure* (1939). His life was dogged with controversy, condemnation (because of his homosexuality), bouts of depression and financial precariousness. Although he had written a large part of the text of *Punishment and Social Structure* between 1931 and 1935, the manuscript was eventually handed over for revisions to Otto Kirchheimer, prior to its publication. The changes were made when the Frankfurt School relocated to the USA after the rise of the Nazi party in Germany. The USA had been traditionally hostile to Marxism and it was felt that the manuscript needed to be toned down for its new audience. Rusche died alone and in poverty after poisoning himself with domestic coal gas in October 1950.

Michel Foucault (1926–84) Perhaps the most influential thinker in penology in the last 30 years, Michel Foucault lived a notorious personal life, but wrote some brilliant—although very complicated—work on penology. His main book in penology is *Discipline and Punish* (1977), which continues to be one of the leading works in the field. An inspiration to a whole generation of thinkers, his influence can be divided into two traditions: those who look at disciplinary power and those who focus on his later work on governmentality. Foucault was a penal activist and a staunch critic of the establishment in France, and his work opened up new ways of thinking about penal power. He died of an AIDS-related illness in 1984.

Progress, modernity and civilisation

Theories of punishment and prisons are often linked with ideas of 'civilisation', 'morality' and 'social progress'. In these theories, punishment is seen as evolutionary and is often tied to the notion of 'modernity'.

Modernity is a period in human history that was shaped by the privileging of rationality and reason above emotions. It is tied to the rise of the Enlightenment in the seventeenth century, which privileged secular human knowledge, and scientific, neutral and objective analysis, above religion and folklore.

The rise of modernity is considered by penologists to have had a defining influence on the development of punishment.

Administrative penology

Administrative penology is the official version of prison life. Changes in punishments since the eighteenth century are perceived to have been progressive and underscored by humanitarian reforms. These reforms are considered to have been motivated by benevolence, altruism and efforts to make the penal system more efficient through the application of scientific principles.

> In this 'quintessentially optimistic' world view, the prison is perceived as a sign of progress in both penal administration and the sensibilities of the nation. The emergence of administrative knowledge and practices provided the platform for the birth of the discipline of penology itself.

Administrative penologies provide excellent descriptions and are often well researched. Good examples are Sydney and Beatrice Webb (1922) *English Prisons Under Local Government* and Sir Leon Radzinowicz and Roger Hood (1986) *History of the Criminal Law* (Volume 5). You should read such accounts, but administrative penologists accept implicitly the claims of those they are investigating.

Emile Durkheim

Durkheim believed that society is a moral entity with a reality all of its own, and argued that common beliefs and shared moral sentiments shape what he called the *'conscience collective'*. It was, for Durkheim, immersion into the moral boundaries of the conscience collective that guides interactions and determines human behaviour. Durkheim was also interested in how the social system is protected from those who challenge these wider shared beliefs and values. Durkheim believed that some acts that are against the law (*'crimes'*) and other behaviours that go against the norms of a society (*'deviance'*) can be signs of progress and a healthy society.

Durkheim also argued, however, that there are other 'crimes' that should be denounced, condemned and punished. These social acts are such an outrage to humanity that they can inflict damage to the conscience collective. The whole of society is the victim of these 'crimes'. All 'healthy' members of society are repulsed and offended by 'crime'. For Durkheim, 'crimes' highlighted the fragility, insecurities and weakness of society. The barbarity of the response shows how deeply the moral sensibilities are offended. The weaker the moral order and social integration, the stronger the threat to the social order, and, consequently, the stronger and more extreme the punishment invoked.

> *Durkheim argued that punishment sends a moral message denouncing heinous behaviour, and reinforces the wider constructions of morality and social cohesion. He argued that, while punishments cannot create consensus, they can express condemnation, and reinforce the morality and consensus that already exists.*

Durkheim argued that the form of punishment is linked to the progress that society has made. For Durkheim, primitive societies were characterised by repressive laws. They constituted a small number of individuals for whom social solidarity was based on similarity and who had an extremely punitive psychological disposition. Punishments were extremely severe and offenders were executed in the most awful ways imaginable: stoned; crucified; hanged; hung, drawn and quartered, with parts of their bodies sent throughout the kingdom; hurled from cliffs; crushed beneath the feet of animals. In contrast, advanced societies are heterogeneous, featuring a specialisation of tasks and recognition of mutual interdependence. In a more secure society, punishments become less severe and restitutive laws replace those that are repressive.

> *For Durkheim, a strong, morally legitimate social order requires very little punishment to reinforce social solidarity.*

Hudson (2003) points out that there are a number of criticisms that can be made of Durkheim's thesis. Durkheim is vague about the historical process, in that he does not identify the point at which primitive societies change into advanced societies. Additionally, he provides no intermediary society that features elements of both of these forms of punishment. Durkheim does not fully engage with power and inequality, and the manner in which consent is organised is not explained. Punishments in a 'law and order society' are used to create consensus, rather than to reinforce existing morality, and the conception of hegemony may provide a more plausible explanation. Finally, there is evidence to suggest that we have seen a shift from restitution to repressive forms of punishment in advanced capitalist societies.

Norbert Elias

In his magnum opus, *The Civilising Process*, first published in 1939, Norbert Elias outlines how Western sensibilities have changed since medieval times. Through close readings of etiquette manuals, fictional works, paintings and various other documents of instruction or description, Elias charts, in fascinating detail, changes in table manners, attitudes towards bodily functions, behaviour in the bedroom, habits of washing and cleanliness, and the proper way of addressing strangers.

> *For Elias, the civilising process involves a tightening of the controls that are imposed by society upon individuals and an increased level of psychological inhibition. Elias argues that humans gradually internalise fears, anxieties and inhibitions that are imposed upon them by their parents and their social environment, developing a superego that inhibits the expression of instinctual drives in accordance with the demands of cultural life. This transformation of the human psyche in the civilising process implies that the more civilised a society, the more its inhabitants are repressed.*

David Garland (1990) has provided one of the most influential accounts of how the work of Elias can be applied to penology. Garland argues that, today, a whole range of possible punishments—tortures; maimings; stonings; public whippings—are simply ruled out as unthinkable because they strike us as impossibly cruel and barbaric. In keeping with the demands of a civilised society, the experience of pain is today ushered behind the prison walls.

Similarly following Elias, Dutch penologist Pieter Spierenburg (1984) concentrates on the changing sensibilities that, in a crucial sense, mediated the link between state development and penal history, while English historian VAC Gattrell (1994) makes similar arguments in relation to the end of public executions in England and Wales.

> *Many critics have questioned whether there really has been any progress around penal sensibilities, while other critics have taken exception to the argument that civilisation and penal reforms can only be achieved through the psychical repression of a naturally evil human nature.*

Elias is vulnerable to criticism in relation to his pessimistic vision of the social order and his notion that perceived moral acts are merely examples of psychological conditioning.

Zygmunt Bauman

In one of the most acclaimed books of recent times, *Modernity and the Holocaust* (1989), Bauman argues that the systematic extermination of 20 million people in the Nazi Holocaust was not an aberration, but rather a problem that is central to the functioning of modern civilisations. Bauman points out that modernity facilitates a '*gardening state*' with big visions aimed at the creation of a new and better society. Alongside great progress, modernity can lead to scientifically and rationally conceived genocide—i.e. genocide with the purpose of creating a better and more civilised society.

> For Bauman, the Holocaust would not have been possible without a civilised, rational, bureaucratic modern society weakening the moral basis of human interactions.

Bauman argues that, in this instance, obedience to bureaucratic orders and the dehumanisation of 'the other' neutralised any sense of responsibility, leading to the social production of moral indifference. Most 'normal' bureaucrats involved in the Nazi killing machine were doing administrative duties as part of a rationally and bureaucratically ordered chain. They did not see the end results and relationships were characterised by distance. This distance was both physical, through the division of labour, and psychological, through the depersonalising and devaluing of certain categories of human being. The only escape, for Bauman, is to prioritise our moral and unreciprocated responsibilities for others, and to create a sense of psychic proximity with all fellow humans.

The implications for penology of this analysis are immense. The rational, the bureaucratic and the managerial are still privileged above the ethical, and one of the main groups of people most easily defined as 'vermin' or 'weeds' are those that we imprison. Nils Christie (2000) has most successfully made this connection. The work of Bauman has been criticised, however, because it is difficult to relate his analysis to other, less technocratic, genocides in the twentieth century, and on the basis that his challenge to modern progress may be politically conservative, because it denies the possibility of a better, all-inclusionary alternative. Further, his analysis critiques modernity itself and so is inconsistent with modernist theorists.

Common pitfall   *When considering the work of Bauman, Elias and Durkheim, ensure that you are aware of their very different views on human nature.*

Social divisions and the distribution of punishments

Penologists have also looked at the way in which punishments have been unequally distributed in modern societies among the social divisions of class, 'race' and gender. Problematising the link between 'crime' and the continued existence of the prison, penologists have attempted to uncover the real functions of imprisonment through analysis of political economy, power, patriarchies and the demands of the labour market. These theorists reflect contemporary political traditions such as liberalism, Marxism and feminism.

Liberalism

Liberalism takes the humanitarian visions of penal reformers at face value, but recognises that they had disastrous consequences. This approach is described by Stanley Cohen (1985) as the *'we blew it thesis'*. In a prime example of this tradition, US penologist David J Rothman's *The Discovery of the Asylum* (1971) identified the importance of religion, humanitarianism and benevolence in the development of the asylum in the USA. Rothman argued that the reformers believed that people could be changed through incarceration, yet, in practice, confinement in total institutions was creating greater harm to, rather than helping, inmates.

> In essence, the liberal penological approach provides us with a pessimistic warning from history that benevolence itself should not be trusted.

Critics have claimed that liberalism has failed to learn from past mistakes, holding firm to the belief that penal reforms can work, if only the great humanitarian principles could be correctly implemented on the ground.

Marxism

Traditional Marxists have looked at the political economy of punishment. The most important contribution to Marxist penology is Georg Rusche and Otto Kirchheimer's *Punishment and Social Structure* (2003), originally published in 1939. The book is firmly located within a material economic framework and aimed to uncover *'why certain methods of punishment are adopted or rejected in a given social situation?'* (p. 3). Rusche and Kirchheimer argued that punishment is an independent social phenomenon that has a complex relationship with 'crime'.

> For Marxist penologists, punishments are historically specific and correspond to the given mode of economic production. In conjunction with non-penal institutions of the state, punishments perform a hidden role in the regulation of poverty. Shifts in the organisation of the economy, then, have implications for the form that punishments will take (Rusche, 1933).

Rusche and Kirchheimer identified three historical epochs.

1. **Feudalism in the Middle Ages** *(13th–15th centuries)* Small parochial societies within which the fine was the main punishment.

2. **Mercantilist capitalism** *(16th–18th centuries)* A society featuring a shortage of labour and the adoption of new reclaiming punishments that were based on hard labour.

3. **Industrialisation** *(18th–20th centuries)* Societies experiencing massive population growth, urbanisation, pauperism and the creation of a 'relative surplus population'.

Rusche and Kirchheimer also identified three functions of the prison in the industrialised historical epoch.

1. **Controlling the poor** Under capitalism, human value is intimately tied to labour market value (i.e. employability). When labour is abundant and paid work is scarce, imprisonment is based upon control of the relative surplus population (i.e. the unemployed).

2. **Disciplining the poor** In times during which labour demand is high and the offender is seen as a valuable human resource, the prison becomes a mechanism for disciplining labour reserves so that they will submit to the demands of the labour market.

3. **Deterring the poor** The morality of the poor is perceived by the ruling classes as susceptible to vice. Imprisonment must act as a deterrent to the poor. Criminals must be symbolically excluded as 'less eligible' or less deserving of help than the working poor.

A number of criticisms have been raised against the thesis of Rusche and Kirchheimer. It is often considered to be historically unreliable, because not all capitalist economies developed in the same way. Prisons are very expensive and are not a rational response to labour market economic demands. They ignore ideological constructions of imprisonment and are also accused of being gender-blind, because there is no consideration of the different forms that the social control, regulation and punishment of women can take.

Anti-slavery

J Thorsten Sellin's *Slavery and the Penal System* (1976) follows in the tradition of Rusche and Kirchheimer (1939) and German legal theorist Gustav Radbruch, in his claim that current legal punishments are derived from slavery.

> *Both imprisonment and slavery entail the loss of citizenship, dehumanisation and 'othering', the deprivation of liberty and being forced to undertake manual labour.*

Sellin argues that legal punishments were originally the private domestic punishments of slaves, but that, over the centuries, they have been made applicable to all offenders. He explains that, in ancient civilisations such as the Roman Empire, slavery was legitimated and freemen were exempt from punishments. Hard labour in the imperial metal and salt mines (*'ad metalla'*) or in the chain gangs repairing roads, cleaning sewers and public baths (*'opus publicum'*) became the primary punishment of the poor.

The incorporation of slave punishments into state punishments was also evident in the Middle Ages in Europe. Slavery was firmly established among the Germanic peoples and manual labour was considered beneath the dignity of freemen. Offences by freemen against persons of property were settled by payment of financial indemnities, often without official intervention. But as property relations developed, the dehumanising labour-orientated slave punishments were thought to be appropriate to impoverished freemen unable to purchase immunity.

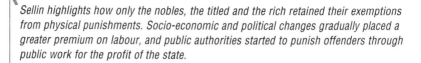

Sellin highlights how only the nobles, the titled and the rich retained their exemptions from physical punishments. Socio-economic and political changes gradually placed a greater premium on labour, and public authorities started to punish offenders through public work for the profit of the state.

Opus publicum (forced public labour) was revived, and was performed both indoors and outdoors in irons. Sellin argues that, by the late sixteenth century, penal slavery was deeply embedded in legal punishments across Europe and its colonies, such as the USA. He places a premium on highlighting how imprisonment is connected to a wider, dehumanised slave condition.

Sellin has been criticised on similar grounds to the Marxist penologists and, specifically, on the basis that his analysis of penal servitude is too broad and geographically disparate.

Neo-Marxism

Steven Box, in his book *Recession, Crime and Punishment* (1987) and in a number of articles co-written with Chris Hale in the early 1980s, provides one of the most impressive neo-Marxist analyses of imprisonment. Box and Hale (1982) challenge the orthodox account of the relationship between unemployment, 'crime' and imprisonment. They argue that official crime rates are not necessarily influenced by unemployment and economic hardship, but that the *belief* that unemployment and 'crime' are intimately connected has significant consequences for who is imprisoned.

*'Neo' means 'new', so **neo-Marxism** simply means 'New Marxism'. For an excellent example of neo-Marxist criminology, see Hall et al. (1978).*

For Box and Hale, in times of recession, the sentence of imprisonment is *'an ideologically motivated response to the perceived threat of crime posed by the swelling population of economically marginalised persons'* (p. 363). Judges believe that unemployment *will* lead to an increase in 'crime' among certain sub-populations of the relative surplus population and consider it to be important to punish the 'sub-proletariat' to send a deterrent message to society. Looking at ideology can help to explain why prison is used when it is clearly not the most rational or cost-effective solution to social problems.

Neo-Marxist approaches are critiqued for being functionalist.

Modernist feminism

Penology has been criticised for being written by men, for men and about men. Male knowledge has been presented as 'the' knowledge.

> Until the 1980s, penological studies largely ignored how the punishment of women is different from that of men. In recent years, feminist penologists have highlighted this theoretical blind spot, detailing the ways in which women are regulated differently from men through informal means of social control and how women experience state punishments very differently from men.

Francis Heidensohn (1985) outlined how women offenders are *doubly* deviant, having broken both legal and gender rules of conduct. Their punishment might be determined by how well they are able to conform to gender expectations and middle-class respectability. Pat Carlen (1983) interviewed women prisoners at Scotland's Cornton Vale prison and outlined how the pains of imprisonment for women were harsher than those of men. This was due to a number of reasons:

- isolation and being miles away from home;
- the creation of dependency through imprisonment;
- being treated like children;
- the use of heavy discipline by staff;
- the expectation of excellence in domestic duties;
- denial of their status as either real criminals or real women.

Many modernist feminists have argued for the need for a 'woman-wise' penology.

Michel Foucault

Michael Foucault's *Discipline and Punish: The Birth of the Prison* (1977) is one of the most influential books in penology in the last thirty years. Taking as his backcloth the change from capital punishment to the timetabled regimes of the penitentiaries, Foucault rejected the liberal argument that the prison was a form of humanitarian progress, claiming instead that prisons developed *'not to punish less; [but] to punish better, to insert the power to punish more deeply into the social body'* (p. 82).

Although he did not reject the 'top-down' Marxist approach of penologists such as Rusche and Kirchheimer, Foucault used a different analytical framework and understanding of how power operates 'bottom up'. He was interested in how disciplinary power impacted on the human soul (the psyche) at the micro level.

> For Foucault, power is productive, dispersed throughout society and intimately related to the construction of knowledge. Foucault wished to understand how the '***power/ knowledge***' axis could be deployed to observe and render human beings obedient.

Hunt and Wickham (1994) explain how, for Foucault, disciplinary power operated on three levels, as follows.

1. ***Hierarchical observation*** Differentiated positions of power that are rooted in surveillance, categorisation and classification.

2. ***Normalising judgements*** Dominant definitions, rules, norms and expected behaviour.

3. ***Micro penalties and rewards*** Means of regulation to ensure conformity and obedience.

The prison was not the only means through which disciplinary power operated—other places included the school, the family and the workplace—but it was at the pinnacle of a 'carceral' continuum.

> To justify wider disciplinary controls, Foucault argues, the prison deliberately invents delinquents. In this sense, a state of permanent conflict exists to meet the needs of a crime control industry and to legitimate wider disciplinary controls. Further, certain illegalities are isolated and made manageable, while some offenders can be retrained and turned into disciplined, docile and productive human beings.

Foucault has been criticised for overgeneralising disciplinary punishments used against juveniles to those used against adults and for providing only a partial analysis of punishments that requires synthesis with one, or more, of the earlier modernist 'total theories'. He has also been criticised on the bases that, like the Marxists, his analysis is functionalist and masculinist, and that his conception of power is simply a restatement of the basic sociological concept of socialisation.

In recent years, some penologists have looked to develop the later writings of Foucault on penal governance. These are often referred to as **governmentality** theorists, of which tradition Malcolm Feeley and Jonathon Simon (1994) are good examples.

"What has been the contribution of feminist studies to our understanding of the role of imprisonment?"

When answering this question, it is important that you identify the main feminist writers on imprisonment, including Pat Carlen, in particular. Specifically, try to highlight how they locate the historical and contemporary punishment of women within wider forms of social control and regulation, and how the needs and pains of women offenders and prisoners have been neglected. Demonstrate knowledge of alternative masculinist penologies, but do not lose your focus on feminist epistemology (i.e., knowledge).

Taking it *FURTHER*

The theories discussed above continue to be relevant to penologists writing today. Below are listed a number of recent books and their connections to the penological traditions discussed above.

Contemporary penologists	Theoretical tradition
Lord Windlesham (1998) Responses to Crime	Administrative penology
Jock Young (1999) The Exclusive Society	Durkheimian
John Pratt (2002) Punishment and Civilisation	Eliasian
Nils Christie (2000) Crime Control as Industry, 2nd edn	Baumanian
David Ramsbotham (2003) Prisongate	Liberalist
Jeffrey Reiman (2007) The Rich Get Richer and the Poor Get Prison, 7th edn	Marxist
Loïc Wacquant (2008) Deadly Symbiosis	Anti-slavery/anti-racism
Christian Parenti (1999) Lockdown America	Neo-Marxist
Kelly Hannah-Moffat (2001) Punishment in Disguise	Feminist
Joe Sim (1990) Medical Power in Prisons	Foucauldian/neo-Marxist
Jonathan Simon (2007) Governing Through Crime	Foucault/governmentality

Textbook guide

CAVADINO, M AND DIGNAN, J (2007) *The Penal System*, 4th edn, London: Sage

COHEN, S (1985) *Visions of Social Control: Crime Punishment and Classification*, Cambridge: Polity Press

GARLAND, D (1990) *Punishment and Modern Society: A Study in Social Theory*, Oxford: Oxford University Press

GARLAND, D AND YOUNG, P (EDS) (1983) *The Power to Punish: Contemporary Penality and Social Analysis*, Oxford: Heinemann Education Books Ltd

HUDSON, BA (2003) *Understanding Justice*, 2nd edn, Milton Keynes: Open University Press

MELOSSI, D (ED) (1999) *The Sociology of Punishment*, Aldershot: Ashgate

2.3

sources of penal knowledge

Core areas: **telling secrets**

lies, damn lies and official prison statistics

official reports and inquiries

the media: more bad news?

penal pressure groups and the unions: acceptable penal critics?

views from below: novels, biographies and films

the academy: appreciative or critical research values?

Running themes

- Legitimacy
- Pains of imprisonment
- Power to punish

Telling secrets

Prisons are closed, secretive worlds in which it is difficult to uncover the truth. As a student of penology, you need to understand how such state organisations work, what problems they encounter and whether they undertake their functions correctly. Yet you may find that, when researching state institutions, you uncover contradictory evidence, competing or even unsubstantiated knowledge claims, or are told that little or no data is available. This lack of 'visibility' presents major obstacles. Uncovering the truth about prison life requires you to ask the right questions and access the most relevant and contemporary sources. In this chapter, we look at the strengths and weaknesses of the main forms of penal knowledge that are available to help you in your task.

You should try to use all of the sources detailed in this chapter, especially if you are undertaking a penology dissertation.

Lies, damn lies and official prison statistics

The government regularly produces detailed official statistics on prisons and other forms of punishment in society. The Home Office, the Ministry of Justice, the National Offender Management Service (NOMS) and the Prison Service all publish official data. Official prison statistics are an important source of information, but they are not designed, compiled or written in the interests of the general public; rather, they are written as records of the activities, budgets and workloads of state agencies.

Official prison statistics provide data on:

- the 'crimes' of offenders sentenced to imprisonment;
- the social backgrounds of prisoners;
- prison numbers and populations (annual receptions into custody, daily prison populations, population per 100,000 in England and Wales and international comparisons);
- size of the penal estate, costs and staffing;
- key performance indicators (such as data on overcrowding, educational attainments, escapes, health care, violence, drug treatments, suicides and self-harm, or time out of cell);
- recidivism, reconviction rates and known reoffending.

Figure 2.1   The life of a prison statistic

There are a number of reasons why using official prison data is important. Official data:

- provides a (limited) form of penal accountability and means of visibility;
- provides a useful means of measuring state activities;

- indicates why government develops certain priorities, policies and deployment of resources;
- indicates success or failure of policies.

> **Common pitfall** *Over-reliance on official sources may lead to work that is uncritical. Statistics can be easily manipulated, and you must always look to alternative accounts to assess the relevance and accuracy of any statistics.*

Official prison statistics are not, then, objective and impartial accounts, but 'social constructions' of reality, reflecting the interests, goals and objectives of the gatekeepers of state institutions. They are a very useful source of knowledge, but are, at best, only partial accounts of prison life. There are many reasons why official data is limited. First, there are problems that are methodological (i.e. relating to how data is produced) and epistemological (i.e. relating to the limitations of quantitative data). Other concerns arise in terms of accuracy and the differences between reported data, recorded data, and what acts and events really occurred. Matthews (1999) informs us that such difficulties include:

- errors (data wrongly or falsely collated);
- 'dark figures' and omissions (no data or acts remain hidden);
- problems of 'categorisation';
- slippage (redefinition of what is measured);
- telescoping (overcounting).

> *Although academic penologists heavily criticise official statistics, very few do not use them at all.*

Official reports and inquiries

Official reports and inquiries are often written by respected members of the establishment, such as senior police officers, members of the judiciary or senior officers in the armed services. Recent examples of official inquiries include:

- the 1991 report of senior judge Lord Justice Woolf on the serious prison riots that occurred in England and Wales in April 1990;
- the report by Admiral Sir John Learmont on prison security, published in 1995;
- the report published in 2006 by the judge Justice Keith into the murder of Zahid Mubarek on the night before his release from prison.

Checklist of facts to ascertain when looking at an official inquiry

✓ Circumstances in which the report was commissioned.
✓ Authors and advisers.
✓ Timescale, administrative support and legal powers.
✓ Terms of references and interpretation.
✓ Methodology.
✓ Range of people involved and those given greatest credibility.
✓ Recommendations and response of the government.

Official reports are normally presented as open and *'entirely independent of government'* (Keith, 2006, p. 9), apparently providing a thorough, objective, comprehensive and impartial account of events. But official reports represent and promote a particular world view. This 'view from above' influences the definitions and scope of the problem investigated, and the possible means of its resolution. As a result, certain ways of approaching social problems are presented as legitimate, while others are de-legitimated and marginalised as 'irrational'.

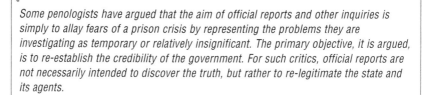

Some penologists have argued that the aim of official reports and other inquiries is simply to allay fears of a prison crisis by representing the problems they are investigating as temporary or relatively insignificant. The primary objective, it is argued, is to re-establish the credibility of the government. For such critics, official reports are not necessarily intended to discover the truth, but rather to re-legitimate the state and its agents.

The media: more bad news?

The term 'media' refers to mass communication systems with large audiences, such as the Internet, radio, television, film and newspapers. There are often very interesting programmes, documentaries or debates about punishment on television or on the radio and many newspapers, such as *The Guardian* or *The Independent*, have dedicated prison correspondents who provide detailed discussions of prison life. To some extent, we are reliant on the media for keeping us informed of events that happen beyond the scope of the informal mechanisms that grant us access to knowledge or of own personal experiences.

The media are also an important source of penal knowledge because they:

- can visibilise a hidden world;
- are an easy way of accessing knowledge;
- can be a means of shaming the government, providing forms of accountability and politicising controversial penal practices;
- can present data in a straightforward manner;
- can provide an up-to-date account.

Common pitfall *Remember that the news is competitive and commercial, with the main intention of making money. The tension between providing information and the need to make stories entertaining can lead to attention being diverted away from certain serious issues to more superficial events or sensationalist takes on stories.*

Although the media is fractured, with each different media group in direct competition the others, it is clear that certain stories and interpretations centred on 'crime' and punishment become dominant, and play a key role in the production and reproduction of current ways of thinking about social problems. In this sense, the media both reflect and perform a key role in shaping the construction of penal realities. In short, media stories are *socially constructed* around certain identifiable newsworthy criteria. Prison stories are patterned and must be immediate, dramatic and simple and, most of all, there must be a means of access to knowledge.

The relationship between the media and prison authorities is institutionalised and access to official sources becomes structured, shaping, in effect, the remits of stories and the level of media critique.

The media sets the agenda, prioritises contrasting accounts, selects the narrator of events, and privileges certain voices and forms of interpretation. Often, the accounts of prisoners are seen as neither credible nor reliable, and so it is penal authorities that exclusively shape the agenda, leading to the reinforcement of dominant values and common-sense assumptions on prison life.

*This dominant world view is sometimes referred to by penologists as **hegemony** or the **hegemonic vision**.*

A certain story may be reconstructed or repackaged into a given media formula that, although not quite fiction, is hardly a true reflection of events. Finally, the media do not provide context to their stories; rather, they present a specific narrative that underscores penal stories that isolate prisoner actions or protest. This narrative leads to constructions of prisoner resistance and dissent as illogical, pointing to the costs or damage caused, rather than as a rational response to a dehumanising lived reality.

> *Compare and contrast stories on prisons in different newspapers and written by different journalists. Look for both the similarities and also the differences between the representations of a single prison story.*

Penal pressure groups and the unions: acceptable penal critics?

Penal pressure groups provide an alternative to government agencies as a source of knowledge and expertise. There are four main groupings:

- the liberal penal lobby;
- the conservative penal lobby;
- the radical penal lobby;
- the staff unions.

The liberal penal lobby

Although by no means homogenous, the liberal penal lobby have traditionally had the 'ear of the government'. Liberal reformers often have good relations with government officials, politicians and civil servants, but these personal connections have sometimes diluted their ability to be critical. The liberal penal lobby provides the core of the credible and acceptable humanitarian voice, selectively critiquing or supporting the Prison Service. There are three main liberal pressure groups.

- **The Howard League for Penal Reform** The Howard League has a very long history and is the most established penal reform group in the United Kingdom. In 1866, The Howard Association was established and took its name from the penal reformer John Howard. The aim of the Howard Association was the '*promotion of the most efficient means of penal treatment and crime prevention*' (www.howardleague.org). In 1907, the Penal Reform League was founded, merging with the Howard Association to form the Howard League for Penal Reform in 1921. Until the late 1970s, the Howard League was largely based around London and, traditionally, aimed to develop close relationships with government officials, rather than to present a radical critique of prisons. Its core beliefs are to work for a safe society in which fewer people are victims of crime and that offenders should make amends for what they have done. In recent decades, the Howard League has looked to adopt a more critical stance and has brought legal challenges under the Human Rights Act 1998, including the very significant case in which it applied the responsibilities of local authorities under the Children Act 1989 to child custody. The League has also campaigned vigorously against the imprisonment of women, suicides and self-injury, overcrowding and poor prison conditions.

- **The Prison Reform Trust (PRT)** The PRT is a relatively recent liberal penal pressure group, established only in the late 1980s. The PRT aims to ensure that prisons in England and Wales are *'just, humane and effective'* (www.prisonreformtrust.org.uk). The PRT believes that prisons should be run by the public sector, and should be open and accountable institutions that are reserved for only the most serious offenders. It believes that prison regimes should be constructive, safe and decent, and should prepare prisoners for resettlement in the community. Recent campaigns have looked to improve conditions, to promote human rights and diversity, to support prisoners' families and to promote alternative community sanctions.

- **Penal Reform International (PRI)** PRI is an international non-governmental organisation that looks to promote the development and implementation of international human rights instruments in relation to law enforcement and prison conditions, to reduce all forms of discrimination and to reduce prison numbers through the promotion of community alternatives. PRI works in partnership with, and is funded by, national governments and intergovernmental organisations such as the United Nations and the Council of Europe. It aims to provide global support, training and expertise for penal reformers. Recent campaigns have focused on prison privatisation, prison overcrowding, transnational justice, pretrial detention and the abolition of the death penalty.

The conservative penal lobby

The conservative penal lobby is not as established as its liberal counterpart, although, in recent times, it has arguably been more influential on penal policy. Right-wing think tanks, such as the Adam Smith Institute, the Institute for Economic Affairs and Civitas, have published politically significant work on prison privatisation, the aims and justifications of imprisonment, and the relationship between 'crime' and imprisonment rates.

The radical penal lobby

Much of the penal knowledge with which we are presented reflects the interests of the powerful. There are very few alternative sources of knowledge that are not, in some way or other, connected with, or reliant upon, those who promulgate the 'view from above'. The radical penal lobby provides an alternative voice and, although relatively few in number and often starved of resources, radical pressure groups continue to provide an independent analysis of government penal policies, practices and organisations.

- **No More Prison** No More Prison was established by John Moore in January 2006, following a successful penal abolition conference, and was conceived as a direct descendent of the abolitionist penal pressure group Radical Alternatives to Prison, which was formed in 1970, but had dissolved by the late 1980s. No More Prison states, in its 'Aims', that:

> Prisons are failed institutions that do not work. They are places of pain and social control and are brutal, abusive and damaging to everyone who is incarcerated in them. Prisons are fundamentally flawed and all attempts to reform them have failed. We are committed to their abolition through:
>
> - Exposing the reality of imprisonment today;
> - Stopping the building of new prisons and the expansion of existing prisons;
> - Highlighting the fact that prisons not only fail prisoners but also have a negative impact on families and friends, victims and survivors and the whole community;
> - Campaigning to close existing prisons;
> - Opposing the criminalisation of young people, working class and minority ethnic communities;
> - Promoting radical alternatives to prison that focus on social and community welfare rather than punishment.
>
> (www.alternatives2prison.ik.com)

- **INQUEST** INQUEST is a charitable organisation that was formed in 1981 by the families and friends of those who have died in custody. It works for '*truth, justice and accountability*' (www.inquest.gn.apc.org), and provides both advice and support to the families of those who have died in custody. INQUEST campaigns and monitors issues surrounding deaths in custody (police, prison, immigration detention and deaths of detained patients) throughout the United Kingdom. INQUEST looks to campaign at Westminster for changes in inquest procedures and changes in the law, but perhaps most importantly, it provides specialist, free, confidential and independent support to those who have been bereaved.

- **Women In Prison (WIP)** WIP was formed by ex-prisoner Chris Tchaikovsky in October 1983 to campaign specifically around women's imprisonment. WIP points out that, because there are relatively fewer women than men in prison, the differential sentencing, experiences, pains and discrimination of women have been largely ignored or marginalised among mainstream penal pressure groups. Chris Tchaikovsky died in 2002, but WIP continues to struggle for justice for women in the courts, prison and after release.

> *Penal pressure groups should be an indispensable source of your information. They generally provide up-to-date commentaries on government policy. Many penal pressure groups have also published books or have information on current penal controversies. You are strongly advised, whatever level or focus of your study, to look regularly at their websites and at their publications (such as the Howard Journal).*

The staff unions

Prison officers and governors also have specific pressure groups that promote their interests and lobby government. These are organised as trade unions.

- **The Prison Officers' Association (POA)** The POA has a membership of 33,500, and represents all prison officers and governor grades 4 and 5 in public sector prisons in the United Kingdom. It also has a large number of members in private prisons. The POA aims to protect and to promote the interests of its members, to improve working conditions and to provide free initial legal advice.
- **The Prison Governors Association (PGA)** The PGA has a much smaller membership than that of the POA and represents more senior grades of governor. The PGA works in the interests of the governors, who have much better pay and conditions than those of prison officers, and its current union president is Paul Tidball.

Views from below: novels, biographies and films

Penologists who focus upon the 'view from below' privilege the knowledge of the powerless, and how they interpret and define their experiences. In this sense, the view from below can provide:

- an accurate and true account of offenders' everyday lived experiences;
- an insight into offender meanings and motivations;
- a platform for the voice of the disempowered (emancipating subjugated knowledge);
- initiation of an alternative source of legitimate knowledge;
- a means of turning personal struggles into public issues.

There are a number of fictional accounts that help us to understand the experiences of prisoners. Two of the most influential are by famous Russian novelists. Theodore Dostoevsky's *House of the Dead* (1860) and Alexander Solzhenitsyn's *One Day in the Life of Ivan Denisovich* (1963) provide highly descriptive and moving accounts of the pains of confinement. Both of these books are partially based on the authors' own experience of penal servitude. Many other ex-prisoners have written about their experiences: Jimmy Boyle's *A Sense of Freedom* (1977), Mark Leech's *A Product of the System* (1992) and Ruth Wyner's *From the Inside* (2003) are good examples.

There are also many films that have looked to uncover the prisoners' world view. Some of the best of this genre are: *Scum* (1979); *Brubaker* (1980); *Ghosts of the Civil Dead* (1988); *The Shawshank Redemption* (1994); *Carandiru* (2003).

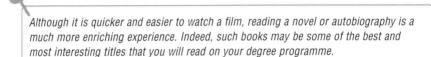

Although it is quicker and easier to watch a film, reading a novel or autobiography is a much more enriching experience. Indeed, such books may be some of the best and most interesting titles that you will read on your degree programme.

The academy: appreciative or critical research values

The final important source of penal knowledge is that of academics—but what are very important to consider when turning to this source are the research values of the penologist and the questions that are asked.

There are two broad approaches to undertaking penological research: appreciative inquiry and critical inquiry. Alison Liebling (2004) is the leading proponent of AI. She claims that AI provides a faithful or truthful account of the respondent's positive achievements, survival strategies and success stories, alongside his or her negative experiences. Because the approach is future-orientated, rather than focused only on the present or the past, outcomes and methodology are intimately tied.

Questioning is appreciative in that, as a mode of inquiry, it asks that a respondent dwells on the *best* as well as the worst aspects of his or her prison experience. Interview questions focus on 'prison values' and are very specific. Respondents are asked to provide evidence of answers by way of an example, illustration or story drawn from his or her actual experiences. AI claims to provide a more sensitive, nuanced and instructive picture of the prison, and thus a more valuable approach than that of the traditional problem-orientated studies.

A number of criticisms have been made against AI:

- it does not uncover the truth and fails to highlight any real negative aspects of imprisonment;
- it is not really a research method;
- it is too closely tied to government agents and the researcher can become a 'technician of the powerful'—i.e. his or her research can be manipulated to support the interests of the government.

By contrast, critical inquiry is independent and asks difficult questions that look to uncover the truth, in a way that potentially challenges the interests of the powerful. Prison research should always aim to uncover real life, whatever this may look like. As Charles Wright Mills (1959) argues:

> Any style of empiricism involves a metaphysical choice—a choice as to what is most real ... One tries to get it straight, to make an adequate statement—if it's gloomy, too bad; if it leads to hope, fine.
>
> (pp. 67, 78)

As a metaphysical choice, it seems more appropriate to allow the respondents to detail their stories, whether positive or negative, so that their construction of events and reality can be outlined and critically interrogated. In critical inquiry, there is no great aim to change the future prison *through the research process*, but rather the more modest aim of simply getting to the 'truth'. Such independent findings might not necessarily be good, or positive, but at least they are an account of actual experiences and illustrate their interpretive framework.

> *Always try to uncover the theoretical and research priorities of the authors of a given study. This will help you to understand the kind of questions they have asked and also to contextualise their findings.*

" Is there a crisis of penal visibility? "

This question asks you to consider the argument made by Mike Fitzgerald and Joe Sim (1982) that the truth about the brutal realities of prison is becoming more visible. You will need to consider how much information about prison gets into the public arena, especially through the media. You may wish to conclude by considering how this information impacts upon public opinion and acknowledgement of prisoner dehumanisation. Stan Cohen's *States of Denial* (2001), and Cohen and Laurie Taylor's *Prison Secrets* (1978), will help you to contextualise the public response to the often unwelcome knowledge of prison life.

Taking it **FURTHER**

You may wish to look up an official report on the Prison Service and see how it presents the 'truth' about prison life. One recent official inquiry on prisons is the Keith Report, published on 29 June 2006. This report investigated Robert Stewart's violent attack on his '*pad mate*' Zahid Mubarek on the night before Zahid was due to be released from Feltham Young Offender Institute. Zahid died eight days later, on 28 March 2000.

Although the chairman of the inquiry, Mr Justice Keith, adopted an open methodology—holding public hearings, seminars and focus groups, and undertaking an extensive documentary review—he interpreted the terms of reference in a restrictive way. Further, although some prisoner evidence was accepted as reliable, its credibility was generally cast in a negative light. For example, Keith (2006) stated that, with regards to prisoners detailing previous offences and racist beliefs, '[i]*nvariablly what the prisoner says is not reliable ... There is no reason to suppose that prisoners always tell the truth*' (p. 500).

The 88 recommendations of the report largely proposed amendments or greater adherence to existing Prison Service policies, sending a reassuring message that '*much of what would have been recommended is now in place*' and that '*many of the systematic shortcomings this report has laid bare have been eliminated*' (p. 443). Keith did question the evidence of some prison officers, naming and shaming those who he deemed culpable, but was largely supportive of the Prison Service.

Textbook guide

FLYNN, N (1998) *Introduction to Prisons and Imprisonment*, Winchester: Waterside Press

GREEN, S, JOHNSON, H AND YOUNG, P (2008) *Understanding Crime Data*, Milton Keynes: Open University Press

JEWKES, Y (2007b) *Media and Crime*, 2nd edn, London: Sage

JEWKES, Y AND BENNETT, J (2007) *Dictionary of Prisons and Punishment*, Cullompton: Willan Publishing

MATTHEWS, R (1999) *Doing Time*, London: Palgrave

RYAN, M (2005) *Penal Policy and Political Culture*, Winchester: Waterside Press

WALLIMAN, N (2006) *Social Research Methods*, London: Sage

2.4	
comparative penologies	

Core areas: **investigating prison populations: international and comparative studies**

the importance of comparative analysis

the analytical framework of comparative analysis

case studies

learning the lessons?

Running themes

- Human rights
- Labour market
- Less eligibility
- Managerialism
- Pains of imprisonment
- Power to punish
- Social divisions

Table 2.1   Prison populations in 20 countries

Country	Prison population total (No. in penal institutions, incl. pre-trial detainees)	National population	Prison population (per 100,000 national population)
Australia	25,353	20.2m	126
Brazil	361,402	189.2m	191
Chad	3,416	9.7m	35
China	1,548,498	1,308.7m	118*
Colombia	62,216	46.3m	134
Cuba	55,000	11.3m	487
Finland	3,954	5.26m	75
France	52,009	61.16m	85
Germany	78,581	82.5m	95
India	332,112	1,092.3m	30
Italy	61,721	59.32m	104
Japan	79,055	128.2m	62
Netherlands	21,013	16.38m	128
New Zealand	7,620	4.1m	186
Norway	3,048	4.62m	66
Russia	869,814	142.3m	611
South Africa	157,402	47.04m	335
Sweden	7,450	9.06m	82
USA	2,186,230	296.4m	738
Venezuela	19,853	26.9m	74

*Sentenced prisoners only

Investigating prison populations: international and comparative studies

A number of non-government organisations (NGOs) investigate prison conditions and the prisoners' experiences of imprisonment around the world. These include **Amnesty International**, **Penal Reform International** and **Human Rights Watch**. The reports of NGOs are aimed at trying to highlight torture and appalling prison conditions as a means of shaming a given government or of raising consciousness among other nations and their governments.

Common pitfall   *Remember that, although NGO reports have been very effective in achieving many of their aims, they are largely descriptive rather than analytical. Students are not their intended audience. For essays, always complement the information from such organisations with academic work.*

There is also great interest in comparing the numbers of people sent to prison. Roy Walmsley (2006) gives details of prison population rates per 100,000 of the national population in 214 countries. In October 2006, there were more than 9.25 million people held in penal institutions throughout the world. Almost half were held in the USA (2.19 million), China (1.55 million plus pretrial detainees and those in 'administrative detention'), or Russia (0.87 million). Today, the USA has the world's highest prison population rate at 738 per 100,000 of the general population (see Table 2.1).

Statistical comparative studies are limited in terms of their measurement and compilation. Specifically, there are concerns that:

- not all forms of administrative detention are included in official records, so, in many countries, the figures will always be underestimates;
- in some countries, such as those in Eastern Europe, there may not be sufficient statistical information available;
- the data is often collated in different countries at different times or years;
- national populations may be inaccurate and may therefore distort the claimed prison population per 100,000;
- the data looks only at daily populations, and therefore neglects the equally significant annual input and throughput of prisoners.

Common pitfall *Comparative data shares the limitations of other forms of official statistics and should be used guardedly.*

The importance of comparative analysis

The study of comparative penal systems is very important. Cavadino and Dignan (2006) remind us that it helps us to avoid reductionist, deterministic and ethnocentric social analysis. It allows us to understand the similarities, differences and broad trends in the way in which imprisonment has been deployed historically around the globe. It can also help us to understand why changes occur in our country, both through examining the policies of similar countries and through analysing the influence that other penal initiatives have had on our own host country. This is particularly useful when thinking about the growth in prison populations and the decline of the welfare state in many Western countries. Comparative analysis can also be used to examine the complex (if not relatively insignificant) relationship between 'crime' and punishment, the correlations between official crime and prison rates, and similarities and differences in the social backgrounds of prisoners and the offences they have committed. Comparative analysis can either demonstrate the validity of a given theory or illustrate its parochial nature and even its inaccuracy.

Penologists have employed comparative analysis to investigate:

- the social contexts of imprisonment in different countries and to attempt to uncover possible commonalities in social structures, cultures, ideologies or political economies;
- a particular region of the world—for example, nations in the European Union—and to attempt to uncover commonalities, harmonisation and/or differences between penal policies and practices;
- continuities and discontinuities between two or three specific countries;
- the policies of a given country—for example, the USA—to see if similar policies might be adopted by other governments elsewhere;
- the nature and extent of one specific issue—such as deaths in custody, prison labour, drugs, HIV, prison conditions or the legal rights of prisoners— in a number of different countries;
- historical factors and colonial contexts shaping the development of the prison around the world.

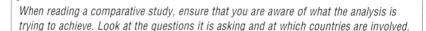

When reading a comparative study, ensure that you are aware of what the analysis is trying to achieve. Look at the questions it is asking and at which countries are involved.

The analytical framework of comparative analysis

Comparative analysis has a number of strands. It is important to remember that these should be adopted for the study of any penal system, including that of England and Wales. Comparative penological analysis provides rich and detailed descriptions of a given nation, and is able to draw out the main configurations that shape the form, nature and extent of punishment in that country at any given moment in time. In so doing, it often aims to:

- compare like with like whenever possible;
- identify continuities and forms of penal convergence alongside differences;
- examine whether similar societies have similar patterns of punishment;
- outline the extent of influence of other countries (such as the USA) on penal policy and practice.

Comparative analysis entails consideration of most of the following factors.

- **Socio-economic** Including: political economy; labour market demands; commitments to welfare state; and fiscal pressures.
- **Governmental** Including: law; criminalisation and age of criminal responsibility; social and penal policies; patterns of punishment; managerialism; aims of imprisonment and penal administration; attitudes of policymakers, politicians, civil servants and penal professionals; and the role of the judiciary and sentencing.
- **Control** Including: the balance between informal social controls, such as family, school, work and community, and formal social controls; and gendered and/or racialised differences in social control.
- **Cultural** Including: specific historical and geographical legacies; societal and penal norms, values and sensibilities; public opinion, the media, and law and order ideology; individualism or collective orientations; and perceived levels of social insecurity and anxiety.
- **Extraterritorial** Including: migration; globalisation; accelerating international information exchange; and foreign national prisoners.

Common pitfall *This list of criteria is useful for thinking about prisons and punishment even when exclusively looking at England and Wales. This is sometimes referred to as* **penality***.*

Some very good examples of comparative penologies that adopt a number of these criteria include Ruggiero et al.'s *Western European Penal Systems: A Critical Anatomy* (1996) and Cavadino and Dignan's *Penal Systems: A Comparative Approach* (2006).

Case studies

Weiss and South (1998, p. 2) argue that there have been five great developments shaping imprisonment in recent times.

1 The rise of neoconservative governance and neoliberal political economy in the West, alongside economic decline, class polarisation and fiscal crisis.

2 The introduction of the market economy in China.

3 The collapse of the Soviet Union and associated Communist regimes.

4 The return to civilian rule in most of Latin America, as well as a renewed push towards privatisation and other neoliberal economic prescriptions.

5 The fall of apartheid in South Africa.

To this list, we might add the following two major developments of the last ten years.

6 The consequences of the US-led war on terrorism and the subsequent increase in global insecurities.

7 The re-emergence of (the visibility of) slavery and human trafficking.

Australia

Australia is a federal state and a former colony of the United Kingdom. It was the destination of over 162,000 British felons between 1787 and 1869, and the contemporary distribution of punishments must be understood within this colonial context. Australia is a country with rising prison populations.

In 1986, there were 70 prisoners per 100,000 of the population. By 1996, the rate had risen to 119, with an average daily population (ADP) of 16,399 adult prisoners. In 2006, this had increased once again to a rate of 126 and an ADP of 25,353 prisoners.

There is no federal penal system and punishments are delivered by the different states of Australia.

Two issues are central to understanding contemporary imprisonment in Australia: the massive difference in rates of incarceration between states and the over-representation of Aboriginal people in prison.

Whereas some states—such as Victoria and South Australia—have comparatively low rates of 60–80 per 100,000, others—such as Queensland,

Western Australia and New South Wales—have rates that double this, standing between 140 and 170. The imprisonment rate of the Northern Territory is twice as high again, at over 390 per 100,000. People of Aboriginal descent make up about 2 per cent of the overall Australian population, but over 20 per cent of the prison population. In the mid-1990s, the imprisonment rate of Aboriginal men was 2,749 per 100,000; for Aboriginal women, the rate stood at 152. In the Northern Territory, Aborigines constitute 70 per cent of the prison population. In general, Australian states with high Aboriginal populations tend to have higher rates of imprisonment.

How has the aboriginal population been affected by their high rates of incarceration.

Brazil

Brazil is a federal republic with 26 states. Around 45 per cent of the Brazilian population live in extreme poverty, with 69 million people earning less than $100 per month. Many of the poor live in slums (*'favelas'*). In 1834, Brazil became the first Latin American nation to build a penitentiary, adopting the idea from the southern states of the USA. Today, there is no federal prison system and therefore penal administration is the responsibility of each given state. The military police are responsible for the external security of all prisons. In 2001, there were 147 military prisons, 100 penitentiaries, 66 public jails and 33 agricultural penal colonies in Brazil.

In 1995, there were 95 prisoners per 100,000 of the population and an ADP of 148,760 prisoners. In 1997, this had increased to 109 prisoners per 100,000 and an ADP of 170,602. By 2006, the rate had rocketed to 191 prisoners per 100,000, an ADP of 361,402. This is an increase of the ADP of over 190,000 in less than ten years.

> *Brazilian prisons are filled with the relative surplus population and their practices are rooted in the doctrine of less eligibility. Ninety six per cent of Brazilian prisoners are men, and they are largely unemployed and sentenced for robbery, theft or drug trafficking. Prisons are acutely overcrowded, with poor hygiene, living conditions and health care.*

Prison labour is low skilled and the profound dehumanisation of prison life has led to an epidemic of sexual violence, mutiny, rebellion and violent escapes, and to deadly clampdowns by the Brazilian military on prisoners and their families.

China

China is a People's Republic and has a population of 1,308.7 million. The Communist Party dominates and has a poor reputation for upholding the human rights of its citizens. In China, strong government is good government. Keeping face is culturally very important, and requires both individuals and the state to appear dignified and in control. In 1978, China 'modernised' and introduced major economic reforms. This not only led to massive economic growth, but also had significant social consequences. There is high labour mobility and massive internal migration of transient populations, with around 50–60 million people per day on the road in China. This migration is coupled with rising unemployment, inflation, crime rates and recidivism.

Incarceration in China is divided between the detention sector and the prison sector. Detentions are organised by the Ministry of Public Security and we do not know exactly how many people are incarcerated. Penal philosophy is linked to 'thought reform' and the transformational role of penal labour, which has roots in the Confucian tradition under which physical labour is understood as a form of enslavement. This tradition was reinforced by the importation of Western penal philosophy in the last dynasty of China in the nineteenth century and by the influence of the Soviet Marxist Gulags in the twentieth century. Until recently, prisoners were leased out to local employers, who were obliged to offer them work after release. To counter claims of slavery, in December 1994, the Chinese renamed 'reform through labour' as imprisonment.

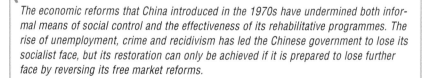

The economic reforms that China introduced in the 1970s have undermined both informal means of social control and the effectiveness of its rehabilitative programmes. The rise of unemployment, crime and recidivism has led the Chinese government to lose its socialist face, but its restoration can only be achieved if it is prepared to lose further face by reversing its free market reforms.

Finland

Finland is a secular and highly bureaucratic social democratic government. Like other Nordic countries (Sweden, Norway, Denmark and Iceland), Finland is heavily influenced by its neighbours. It is a small country with a population of 5.3 million.

Finland's prison rate had dropped from the very high rate of 190 per 100,000 in 1950 to 118 by 1976. From this time, Finland witnessed an unbroken 23-year reduction in imprisonment rates until 1999. The rate stood at 55 in 1995 and fell as low as 46 per 100,000 in 1999. In recent years, however, the prison population has started to increase again, standing at 75 per 100,000 in 2006. The fluctuating imprisonment rate has had little impact on the recorded rate of 'crime' and the Finnish governments have so far been successful in keeping penal policy away from populist political rhetoric (Cavadino and Dignan, 2006).

Japan

Japan is an *'oriental liberal corporatist'* capitalist state (Cavadino and Dignan, 2006) and, in recent times, has had a very low imprisonment rate. Japan is a group-orientated society and citizenship is closely tied to the collective identity of the nation. There is close social integration into families, and both the education system and workplace foster mutual bonds. The Japanese culturally favour informal mechanisms of social control as opposed to penal harshness, and honour, shame, apology and reciprocal obligations to others have special significance in everyday life. The vast majority of Japanese offenders confess and repent, and those offenders who can show a capacity for resocialisation are likely to receive suspended sentences or probation. Japan has very harsh and authoritarian laws, but these are mitigated by the discretionary lenience of practitioners. In this sense, the criminal justice system provides an ideological function that can promote the impression of majesty, justice and mercy.

In 1935, Japan had an ADP of 55,000 prisoners (56 per 100,000). It then reached the very high level of 198 per 100,000 in 1950, before declining to 64 in 1970 and reaching a low of 36 per 100,000 in 1992. In 1999, the prison rate stood at 42 per 100,000 and, by 2002, Japan had an imprisonment rate of 52 per 100,000. In 2006, this had edged up to 62 per 100,000 of the national population, which is nearly double the rate of 14 years earlier.

Prison life is highly regimented and very orderly. Punishments are intended to foster social inclusion and reintegration. The movement of a prisoner, even in his or her cell, is heavily controlled. In 1990, for example, there were only three escapes from Japanese prisons. Prisoners who have tried to escape, or who are perceived as a discipline problem, are made to wear leather or metal restraints that immobilise the movement of their hands.

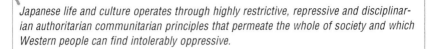

Japanese life and culture operates through highly restrictive, repressive and disciplinarian authoritarian communitarian principles that permeate the whole of society and which Western people can find intolerably oppressive.

South Africa

South Africa is a country that is in transition from an authoritarian apartheid society to one that is rooted in the principles of democracy.

Despite recent changes, South Africa's 47 million inhabitants remain profoundly divided in terms of race, class and power. The political system was transformed when the African National Congress (ANC) gained power in 1994, but post-apartheid South Africa's great divides in wealth and power have not yet been adequately addressed.

In 1980, South Africa had a prison rate of 423 per 100,000: at that time, the highest in the world. In 1995, the official imprisonment rate declined to 273 per 100,000 of the general population. Although many members of the now-ruling party, the ANC, have experienced imprisonment at first hand, this has not led to a concerted effort to reduce imprisonment for the largely poor Black property offenders who are incarcerated. Indeed, by 2006, the rates had crept back up to 335 per 100,000 and an ADP of 157,402 prisoners.

USA

The USA is the most advanced capitalist and the richest nation on earth; it also has the largest prison population. It is an economic and cultural leader, and this 'imperialism' can also be seen in terms of penal policy. In the late 1960s, US President Richard Nixon adopted a tough 'law and order' ideology that has led to an increase in prison populations since the mid-1970s that is unprecedented in a democratic society. This expansionism was further fuelled by the 'war on drugs' that was initiated by President Ronald Reagan during the 1980s.

In 1980, 19 people out of every 1,000 people arrested for drug offences were sent to prison. By 1992, this had increased to 104. The USA's ADP of prisoners stood at 744,208 in 1986. By 1998, it had reached 1,725,842 prisoners. In February 2000, the USA ADP broke the 2 million mark and, by 2006, it had continued to rise to 2,186,230. This leaves the USA with an imprisonment rate of 737 prisoners per 100,000 of the general population. In 2006, the number of people under correctional supervision (i.e. in prison, on probation or on parole) was 6.9 million—over 3 per cent of the population. Louisiana had the highest incarceration rate (795), while Minnesota had the lowest (142). About half of the US prison population is made up of African Americans, although they constitute only 13 per cent of the general population.

One in three young Black men are currently in prison, on parole or on probation. Black American men are eight times more likely to be imprisoned than are White Americans and, if current trends continue, a staggering 29 per cent of Black American men born today will end up in prison at some point during their lifetime.

A number of penologists in the USA have pointed out the continuities between slavery and imprisonment, and how the rich are getting richer, while the poor only get prison (Reiman, 2007).

Venezuela

Venezuela had one of the worst reputations for the treatment of prisoners in the 1990s. Like many Latin American nations, it held a large number of pretrial detainees, with prisoners awaiting trial for an average of three years. The armed forces ran the penal system, and prisons were filled with prisoners accused of drug-related offences, terrorism and offences 'against public security'. In 1992, the ADP was at least 29,000, with a capacity of just over 15,000. In this period, not even Venezuela's Director of Prisons knew how many people were in prison. There was massive overcrowding and, to compound this, prison conditions were very poor and violence was endemic: Venezuelan prisons had the greatest known number of prisoners killed daily in the world.

In recent years, there have been major political changes in Venezuela and the prison population has decreased. In 2006, the ADP was officially 19,853, with an imprisonment rate of 74 per 100,000.

Despite some progress, many of the serious problems that plagued the Venezuelan penal system in the last century remain.

Learning the lessons?

Comparative analysis can lead us to a greater understanding of the forms that punishment is currently taking and what factors may underscore current trends. This can lead us to certain conclusions about the justifications, use, nature and extent of imprisonment.

1 'Crime' has been politicised by all mainstream parties, especially right and centre-left politicians.

2 There is a worldwide increase in the use of imprisonment as a solution to social problems.

3 Imprisonment rates are relatively independent of 'crime' rates.

4 Imprisonment is increasingly being used as a means of stigmatising and controlling non-productive labourers and migrant workers.

5 Punishments are directed against the poorest people in the world.

6 Penal labour and prison work/profitability are central to penal debates.

7 Less eligibility continues to feature in moral discourses on state responsibilities for the incarcerated.

8 There has been a cheapening of human value and a denial of human rights.

9 Sentences have the greatest impact on prison numbers.

10 There has been bifurcation of penal policies and a rise of selective incapacitation.

11 An increase in insecurity and fear has been seen in wider society, along with increases in forms of security when dealing with prisoners.

12 There has been a hardening of penal philosophy, a decline in liberalism and growing intolerance of the poor and non-productive labour.

13 Public sentiments and penal cultures may form a key link between political economy and penal expansionism.

14 There has been a growth of managerialism.

15 Greater penal privatisation has been the norm.

16 The use of repression and the rolling back of the welfare state has been favoured over redistribution, while more authoritarian forms of control have become more deeply embedded.

17 There is evidence of link between penality and different types of political economy: the harsher the social exclusion under political economy, the harsher the punishment.

18 There is massive evidence that the penal solution is, in fact, both irrational and counterproductive.

" Have we seen a greater harmonisation and intensification of penal sanctions in Western European nations? "

This question is looking at a particular region, i.e. at Western Europe. When answering, ensure that you identify the key countries in this region, and then examine their similarities and differences in penal policies, imprisonment rates and forms of social control. You should try to highlight both continuities and dis-continuities. The work of Ruggiero et al. (1996) is indispensable, but good students will also look at more recent data and debates available in journals and from organisations such as Statewatch, as well as conducting a detailed Internet search on the different countries involved.

Taking it *FURTHER*

Take an in-depth look at the rates of imprisonment and forms of punishment in three different countries. Follow the guidance for selection identified in this chapter. Then compare them back to your home country. Think about what this exercise tells you about penology in other countries and in your own.

Textbook guide

CAVADINO, M AND DIGNAN, J (2006) *Penal Systems: A Comparative Approach*, London: Sage

RUGGIERO, V, RYAN, M AND SIM, J (EDS) (1996) *Western European Penal Systems: A Critical Anatomy*, London: Sage

STERN, V (1997) *A Sin Against the Future*, Harmondsworth: Penguin

VAN SWAANINGEN, R (1997) *Critical Criminology: Visions From Europe*, London: Sage

VAN ZYL SMIT, D AND DUNKEL, F (EDS) (2001) *Imprisonment Today and Tomorrow: International Perspectives on Prisoners' Rights and Prison Conditions*, 2nd edn, London: Kluwer Law International

WALMSLEY, R (2006) *World Prison Populations List*, London: ICCPP

WEISS, R AND SOUTH, N (EDS) (1998) *Comparing Prison Systems: Toward A Comparative and International Penology*, Amsterdam: OPA

2.5

the history and aims of imprisonment

Core areas: **the Bloody Code**
the age of reform
the 'great experiment'
the aims of imprisonment in the twentieth century
the history and aims of imprisonment in Northern Ireland and Scotland

Running themes

- Human rights
- Less eligibility
- Managerialism

- Penal reform
- Rehabilitation

Key penologists

John Howard (1726–90) A wealthy aristocrat with profound religious conviction, Howard became Sheriff of Bedfordshire in 1773. He undertook detailed inspections of jails under his jurisdiction and, later, of a further hundred prisons across the country. In 1777, he published his exhaustive study, *The State of the Prisons in England and Wales*. Howard revealed that more people died as a result of appalling prison conditions than were being publicly executed. Howard argued that regular, steady discipline in a penitentiary had the power to turn the '*unhappy wretches*' who broke the law into useful members of society. He was influential in shaping the Penitentiary Act 1779. Howard died of typhus while investigating prison and hospital conditions in the Ukraine in 1790.

Edmund du Cane (1830–1903) Born in Colchester, Sir Edmund du Cane made his reputation organising convict labour in Australia in the 1850s, while still serving in the Royal Engineers. In the 1860s, he became chairman of the board of directors of convict prisons and, from 1877, headed the prison system throughout England and Wales. The architect of Wormwood Scrubs, du Cane was a harsh disciplinarian and presided over brutal penal regimes that were rooted in separate confinement, penal servitude and long periods of silence. His controversial reign of terror came to an abrupt end in 1894.

Lord Justice Woolf (born 1933) Born in Newcastle upon Tyne, Harry Woolf is the son of a builder and architect. One of England's most senior judges, he was appointed to the High Court in 1979 and was Lord Chief Justice from 2000 until 2005. He has been a major figure in promoting liberal penal reform since he conducted a major inquiry into prison disturbances in April 1990. In the subsequent report and in later speeches, Woolf has criticised inhumane prison conditions and overcrowding. His promotion of a balance between '*security, control and justice*' continues to influence liberal penologists.

The Bloody Code

The historian assembles data and is even more aware than the physical scientist how inadequate his [sic] data are. Much of the evidence on which we could base our knowledge of the past has either been destroyed or was never recorded. We guess from the few remaining fragments much as geologists reconstructs a prehistoric monster from a single bone.

(Taylor, 1968, p. 11)

In England in 1166, King Henry II issued the Assize of Clarendon, which ordered his sheriffs to build a jail in each county. Jails held debtors and felons awaiting trial. In 1556, the first 'house of correction' was established at Bridewell and, in 1609, James I made such houses of correction (popularly referred to as 'Bridewells') obligatory in every English county. These facilities held people who were sent to prison for very short sentences.

Alongside this, the workhouse enshrined the principle of less eligibility and was intimately linked to birth of the prison. The control of women rulebreakers was different from that of men. Women were controlled largely through informal patriarchal social controls, but, in terms of the development of penal institutions, the nunnery was a crucial instrument in disciplining deviant, rebellious and sexually promiscuous women.

The scolds bridle

The 'scolds bridle' was used when a woman publicly challenged or insulted her husband. The woman was forced to wear a bridle, which involved a metal cage that was placed around the woman's head. A small pallet with a spike in it was inserted under the woman's tongue. If she attempted to speak her tongue would become impaled on the spike. The woman could then be publicly humiliated, placed in stocks and pelted with rotten vegetables, etc.

In 1750, England was a small parochial society and its population stood at 6.5 million. Seventy-five per cent of the population lived in the countryside and three-quarters worked in agriculture. Local landowners were often the local magistrates and these enforced the law. At this time, there were over 200 separate Acts that commanded the penalty of death (by public hanging). This system of laws and punishments has become known as the 'Bloody Code'.

Despite its apparent barbarity, however, only about 10 per cent of people sentenced to death were actually executed. For historian Douglas Hay (1975), the Bloody Code was really an ideological system of social control combining:

- **majesty** i.e. the power and authority of the law;
- **justice** everybody could be prosecuted under the rule of law;
- **mercy** local elite gained pardons through petitions to the monarch.

Alongside public hangings, the Transportation Act 1718 introduced the transportation of offenders and, from 1718 to 1775, over 30,000 people were transported to the USA. The US War of Independence ended this practice, but, 12 years later in 1787, transportation was reintroduced. From 1787 to 1869, 162,000 people were transported to Australia.

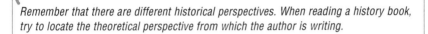

Remember that there are different historical perspectives. When reading a history book, try to locate the theoretical perspective from which the author is writing.

The age of reform

In the eighteenth century, there were a number of significant changes that undermined the Bloody Code. Industrialisation, urbanisation and massive population growth transformed the old agricultural and parochial system. By 1800, the population stood at 15 million and an anonymous society was being formed that was not beholden to the local gentry.

Stan Cohen (1985, p. 13) argues that, during this period, new master patterns of social control developed. These comprised:

- increasing involvement of a centralised state;
- increasing classification of deviants by experts;
- increased incarceration of deviants into 'asylums'—i.e. penitentiaries, prisons, mental hospitals and reformatories;
- the mind replaced the body as the object of penal repression.

The context to the development of these master patterns of control included:

- structural changes in society and the political economy;
- a perceived rise in 'crime' and the threat to order;
- a belief that immorality was the cause of 'crime';
- ideological commitment that prison could reform offenders.

There was a change in emphasis from elimination to reclamation and a rise in the belief that new 'reformed prisons' could act as a 'technology of salvation'.

*Two diametrically opposed philosophies developed. On the one hand, **Christian** reformers believed in the concepts of original sin and the universality of guilt. Immorality was to be rectified by manipulating the shameful offender, using isolation in a prison cell as a condition under which he or she might reflect on, and repent of, his or her unrighteousness. **Utilitarian** philosophers, on the other hand, pleaded for the universality of reason and that reformation could only take place through the socialisation of the offender's proclivity for pleasure. This would be achieved by constant inspection.*

The 'great experiment'

The Hulk Act 1776 was the first move towards a convict prison and the principles of reformation. These 'floating hells' were rife with disease and many prisoners lost their lives in these miserable wooden coffins. William Eden, Willan Blackstone and John Howard introduced the Penitentiary Act 1779.

The Penitentiary Act 1779

William Blackstone sums up the principles of this legislation:

In framing the plan of these penitentiary houses, the principle objects were sobriety, cleanliness and medical assistance by a regular series of labour, by solitary confinement during the intervals of work and some religious instruction to preserve and amend the health of the unhappy offenders and to injure them to the habits of industry, to guard them from pernicious company, to accustom them to serious reflection and to teach them both the principle and practices of every Christian and moral duty.

(1779, cited in Ignatieff, 1978, p. 94)

These reforms had been introduced in response to the end of transportation to the USA and, when transportation to Australia started, the reform movement lost some momentum. In 1810, however, Samuel Romily argued that the Penitentiary Act should be resurrected. The government responded by appointing the Holford Committee (1810), which recommended that a convict prison should be built. It was to be placed at Millbank, on the River Thames in London (McConville, 1995).

The General Penitentiary at Millbank

The General Penitentiary cost £0.5 million and was designed to hold 1,000 prisoners. This *'monument of ugliness'* became a *'maniac-making machine'* (Webb and Webb, 1922, p. 48). In the 1830s, Reverend Daniel Nihil was appointed chaplain governor, and solitary confinement and religious indoctrination became central to the prison regime. The penitentiary proved an unmitigated disaster and was eventually pulled down in 1893.

The convict prison was born, although it had clearly been a hard labour. In 1842, Her Majesty's Prison (HMP), Pentonville, was opened. It held 520 prisoners in separate cells and became the new model prison of the Victorian era. Its regime was based on:

- solitude;
- hard labour;
- religious indoctrination;
- surveillance.

In 1865, the Prison Act finally ended the official difference between 'jails' and 'houses of correction', renaming them 'local prisons' and, in 1877, the Prison Act gave the Home Office control of the prison system. Following this period the modern prison was to become the ultimate sanction of the state.

It is very important that you have a solid grasp of penal history. You will be able to understand the present use of imprisonment much better if you are able to understand its past, so spend some time reading about the development of the prison.

The aims of imprisonment in the twentieth century

Under the guidance of Sir Edmund du Cane, the penal system was harsh, brutal and rooted in the doctrine of less eligibility.

Less eligibility *is predicated on the assumption that there exists a universal free, rational and calculating subject who is infused with an individual sense of responsibility. Criminal activity is understood as a free choice that is based upon weighing up the*

(Continued)

potential benefits and costs of such behaviour. Harsh and punitive regimes will instil moral fibre, discipline and backbone into the criminal, thus eradicating the individual deficiencies that were major factors for his or her offence. The application of the doctrine of less eligibility therefore ensures that the upper margin of prison conditions are guaranteed not to rise above the worst material conditions in society as a whole and so, in times of social hardship, the rigours of penal discipline become more severe to prevent weakening its deterrent effect.

The disciplinary practices of du Cane were eventually challenged when the Gladstone Committee was commissioned. For Gladstone:

> prison discipline and treatment should be more effectually designed to maintain, stimulate, or awaken the higher susceptibilities of prisoners, to develop their moral instincts to train them in orderly and industrial habits, and whenever possible to turn them out of prison better men and women, both physically and morally, than when they came in.

> (1895, cited in Radzinowicz and Hood, 1986, pp. 577–8)

Gladstone did not so much break with the past and the philosophical underpinnings of less eligibility as introduce a new *manifest* task of prison treatment. This new treatment and training ideology had gained ascendancy by the 1920s. Treatment and training focused upon rehabilitation through work, education, physical training and the nurturing of positive staff relationships.

While the treatment and training ideology remained embedded as the orientating rationale of the Prison Service until the late 1970s, there were a number of important official reports on prisons in the 1960s and 1970s that helped to shape the aims of imprisonment during this period. The Mountbatten Report (1966) was written after a number of high-profile escapes and focused on increasing prison security. Mountbatten proposed that all male prisoners should be classified into four categories: A, B, C, or D.

*Mountbatten advocated what is known as a **concentration policy**, which would have placed high-risk prisoners together and allowed much lower security across the rest of the penal estate.*

The Radzinowicz Report (1968) was the report of a subcommittee of the Advisory Council on the Penal System, chaired by Leon Radzinowicz, a Cambridge professor. The committee rejected the concentration policy in favour of what is known as the 'dispersal policy'. Under this policy, Category A prisoners were to be dispersed with Category B prisoners in specially designed high-security training prisons. The adoption of the dispersal policy led to a heightened focus on risk and security across the penal system. Another very important official report of this period was that of the May Committee (Home Office, 1979). Chaired by Judge Mr Justice May, the committee advocated the, now quietly forgotten, notion of 'positive custody'. This proposal was met with official silence and faced devastating criticism from influential penological commentators.

Common pitfall *The recommendations of official reports do not have to be accepted by the government. Some recommendations will become policies, but others are discarded.*

In the early 1980s, a new liberal penological consensus developed in opposition to the doctrines of less eligibility, treatment and training, and positive custody. The consensus was a form of penal realism that was rooted in the principles of 'humane containment'. Humane containment had the modest aim of simply holding those committed to custody by the courts in safe, humane and publicly acceptable living conditions. Penal realism may, unfortunately, accurately sum up about all that is achievable through imprisonment, but such an agenda could hardly provide inspiration for those administering punishments. The '*starkness*' of humane containment led one influential liberal commentator to consider this aim to be '*ontologically insufficient*' (Bottoms, 1990, p. 9).

The liberal penological consensus reached its high tide with the publication of the Woolf Report on the 25 February 1991. Lord Justice Woolf had been commissioned to investigate the disturbances that occurred at HMP Manchester from 1 April – 25 April 1990 and those that occurred at five further institutions: Glen Parva Dartmoor, Cardiff, Bristol, and Pucklechurch. The Woolf Report (1991) is widely regarded as the most significant official report on prisons in England and Wales since the Gladstone Report (1895, cited in Radzinowicz and Hood, 1986, p. 85).

The Woolf Report (1991)

The Woolf report:

- tapped into the logic of the penological consensus and justified imprisonment through the aims of humane containment;
- called for creation of community prisons;
- argued that the Prison Service should balance the key principles of '*security, control and justice*';
- believed that prisons should encourage offenders to take personal responsibility, but that this could only be achieved through facilitating greater opportunities for prisoners to make meaningful choices;
- placed great emphasis on incentives, privileges and legitimate expectations;
- defined prisoners as consumers;
- through advocating prisoner compacts, premised the fulfillment of responsibilities as a perquisite for just, humane containment.

The Woolf agenda has been criticised by Joe Sim (1994) because it:

- worked within the axioms of state-defined penal truth;
- aimed to re-legitimate the prison;
- ignored the experiences of women prisoners;
- ignored wider processes of disciplinary control in society;
- depoliticised prisons by adopting consumerist language.

In 1993, the Prison Service became a 'next steps' agency and the aims of imprisonment were revised to be in tune with the now politically dominant 'managerialist' ethos.

Managerialism promises autonomy, entrepreneurship and innovation, prioritising cost-effectiveness, service efficiency and value for money, while at the same time apparently guaranteeing quality services and products. Promising new flexible and responsive services that can better address the needs of service users, managerialism privileged new rational purposes, goals, mission statements and visions for the prison, and the promotion of new methods to enhance its performance. Under the guise of new public managerialism, the Prison Service developed strategic business plans and targets for monitoring achievement, and commissioned reviews and reports to measure progress and provide evidence of 'value for money'. Importantly, managerialism is framed through a preoccupation with organisational design that is pragmatic and orientated towards action and change—i.e. means rather than ends. Underscoring the logic of managerialism is the privileging of the consumer: the free, rational, empowered and

(Continued)

self-disciplined, self-governing subject is morally responsible for the good or bad choices that he or she makes, and thus for minimising or maximising potential risks. When bad things happen, blame falls squarely on the flawed consumer's shoulders. Further, consumers have only a certain set of entitlements and expectations that are detailed in compacts or contracts, as opposed to the rights and responsibilities of citizens.

Its *Corporate Plan 1993–6* (1993b) provided details of the Prison Service's new managerial vision, goals and values. Alongside this, the Plan also identified eight key performance indicators (KPIs). Remarkably, in the space of only a few years, the Prison Service had shifted from a sense of realism, under which any progressive aims of imprisonment seemed beyond its reach, to the delivery of a plethora of indicators, purposes, visions, goals and values that appeared to have little in common with the aims that had been promoted during the previous decade.

In September 1994, six prisoners escaped from Whitemoor Special Security Unit. The escapees had rope, bullets, two guns, over £400 and a torch. One officer was shot during the escape. Recommendation 62 of the resulting Woodcock Report (1994) emphasised the *'central importance of security in all aspects of activity'* and that all new policies *'should be tested against whether they add to or detract from security standards'*. The government ordered a new inquiry to review security procedures, but its terms of reference were altered by a further politically embarrassing escape: this time by three prisoners, from Parkhurst Prison, Isle of Wight, on 3 January 1995. On this occasion, the escapees had tools, a ladder, a toy gun that fired blanks and a key. The Learmont Report (1995) proposed that prisons should protect the public and deter potential offenders by keeping those sent to them by the courts in *'custody'*; prisons should *'care'* for the prisoner by providing opportunities for him or her to learn from his or her mistakes. It also proposed the development of family ties and the making of redress, along with the *'control'* of prisoners though inducements, based on both incentives and sanctions, and on the better training of prison officers. This renewed emphasis on security was heavily critiqued by liberal commentators as amounting to the creation of new highly repressive and dehumanising iron coffins.

Since 1997, there has been renewed penal optimism that the prison can be a special place in which to rehabilitate and responsibilise offenders. The *Prison Service Strategic Framework* (1998a) provided yet further elaboration of the aims of the Prison Service—this time detailed through aims, objectives and principles.

Aim

- Effective execution of the sentences of the courts so as to reduce re-offending and protect the public

Objectives

- Protect the public by holding those committed by the courts in a safe, decent and healthy environment
- Reduce crime by providing constructive regimes which address offending behaviour, improve educational and work skills and promote law-abiding behaviour in custody and after release

Principles

- Deal fairly, correctly and openly with staff, prisoners and all who come into contact with us
- Work effectively with other bodies
- Help prisoners to take responsibility for their behaviour, to respect the rights of others, to maintain links with their families and the wider community
- Value the contribution of staff, ensuring that they are effectively prepared and supported in the work they do
- Obtain best value from resources provided

The history and aims of imprisonment in Northern Ireland and Scotland

Tomlinson (1996) points out that Northern Irish prisons cannot be understood without consideration of:

- its colonial context;
- the penal system in the whole of Ireland until the 1920s;
- the use of imprisonment during the Troubles from the late 1960s.

Ireland was incorporated in the United Kingdom under the Act of Union in 1800, although it had been subject to British control for a number of centuries. The first prison in Ireland opened in Dublin at Richmond in 1818. After nationalist uprisings, the Anglo-Irish Treaty of 1920 left only Northern Ireland under British rule, but partition did not end the republican struggle. The struggle became increasingly intense in the late 1960s, with the denial of civil rights for Catholic citizens and the murder of unarmed protestors on what became known as 'Bloody Sunday'.

During the Troubles, a number of people were interned (held without trial). In 1975, the Gardiner Committee ended the special status of political prisoners and such prisoners were housed in rapidly built 'H-blocks' at Lomng Kesh, near Belfast, and Magilligan, near Derry. In response, political prisoners refused to wear prison clothes and to wash, and covered their cell walls in human excrement. Out of desperation, republican prisoners embarked on a sustained hunger strike, leading to the deaths of ten prisoners in 1981, including Bobby Sands who had been elected as an MP during these protests. The Good Friday Agreement— signed in April 1998—had a major impact on the Prison Service in Northern Ireland and, from September 1998, led to the release of many paramilitary prisoners. The current aims of the Northern Ireland Prison Service are set out in its vision and values.

Our vision

'To be recognised as a model of good practice in dealing with prisoners and to be valued and respected for our service to the community.'

Our values

- Recognising that the Service requires the commitment of all of us;
- Leading well and behaving with integrity;
- Upholding prisoners' human rights and working with them as individuals to become law-abiding;
- Ensuring that we each have the required skills and competencies;
- Accepting responsibility and accountability;
- Managing resources, including our time, cost effectively;
- Showing an innovative approach to our work;
- Team-working and acting in partnership with other organisations;
- Demonstrating a commitment to fairness, equality and respect for each other and those we are in contact with.

(www.niprisonservice.gov.uk)

Prisons and houses of correction were not as entrenched in Scotland as they were in England and Wales, being fewer in number and housing relatively small numbers of people. Although Bridewells did exist in places such as Glasgow, a correctional system did not develop in Scotland until the 1830s. In 1839, the (Scottish) Prison Act introduced a General Board that undertook the daily administration of prisons and, in 1842, a new 'general prison' was opened at Perth. Later, developments under the Prisons (Scotland) Administration Act 1860 and Prisons

(Scotland) Act 1877 created a centralised system with one penitentiary and 56 county prisons. Remarkably, one of the first steps in the new centralised system was to reduce the number of prisons to 15 by the 1890s. In 1939, the administration of prisons was given to the Secretary of State for Scotland and, until recently, prisons were run by the Scottish Office and Health Department. Today, the Scottish Prison Service is an agency of the Scottish Executive and launched its vision for the future in September 2000: *'We will be recognised as the leader in prisons' correctional work which helps to reduce recidivism and thereby offers value for money for the taxpayer.'*

> The key aims of the Scottish Prison Service (SPS) are custody, order, care and opportunity.

The Scottish Prison Service aspires to meet its aims by concentrating on five key themes:

- Leadership in correctional Service
- A prison estate that is fit for the purpose
- Highest Standards of Service
- Respect for our Staff
- Value for Money for the Taxpayer

(www.sps.gov.uk)

❝ Why did penal reforms continue in the mid-nineteenth century in the face of such obvious humanitarian failure at Millbank and Pentonville prisons? ❞

You should first establish that the early prison reforms were abject failures. Then, consider the arguments for further expansion: identify how prisons are intimately linked with a number of other disciplinary institutions, such as the factory, school, army barracks, the reformed workhouse and the hospital. Also highlight social anxieties and a society that increasingly came to see 'crime' as the result of laziness and degeneracy, and of a dangerous and contagious criminal class that needed to be controlled.

Taking it *FURTHER*

You can download the current aims, values and objectives of the prison services in England and Wales, Scotland and Northern Ireland or read their most recent annual reports and accounts at their websites.

- www.hmprisonservice.gov.uk
- www.niprisonservice.gov.uk
- www.sps.gov.uk

Textbook guide

CAVADINO, M AND DIGNAN, J **(2007)** *The Penal System*, 4th edn, London: Sage

COHEN, S AND SCULL, A (EDS) **(1983)** *Social Control and the State*, Oxford: Blackwell

EMSLEY, C **(1996)** *Crime and Society in England 1750–1900*, London: Longman

MORRIS, N AND ROTHMAN, D **(1998)** *The Oxford History of the Prison*, Oxford: Oxford University Press

RAWLINGS, P **(1999)** *Crime and Power*, London: Longman

SCOTT, DG **(2007)** 'The changing face of the English prison: a critical review of the aims of imprisonment', in Y Jewkes (ed) (2007) *Handbook on Prisons*, Cullompton: Willan Publishing, pp. 49–72

2.6

penal policy

Core areas: **performance and privatisation**

'making punishment work'

cognitive behaviouralism and what works

decency, moral performance and human rights

resettlement and pathways out of crime

Running themes

- Human rights
- Labour market
- Legitimacy
- Less eligibility
- Managerialism
- Rehabilitation
- Risk

Performance and privatisation

A 'performance culture' was first introduced into the Prison Service in England and Wales in 1984. From 1993 onwards, managerial buzzwords and performance monitoring through KPIs and targets, managerial standards and internal audits have had a massive impact on Prison Service policies and practices, and have opened the door to the threat of market testing. Under the principles of 'new public managerialism' (NPM), the capitalist state is transformed from a provider of public services to a 'facilitator' or 'purchaser' of services. Competition in the marketplace and privatisation are perceived as the spurs to innovation, cost effectiveness and value for (taxpayers') money. Through embracing a competitive ethos and new management techniques centring on 'ownership', 'visions' and 'mission statements', existing public sector services are expected to improve their performance significantly. This performance culture and its associated standards are rooted in the requirement of the government to be able to measure, monitor and audit public service outputs. If performance is poor, a competitor can replace the current public service provider.

*The three broad criteria for successful performance revolve around **economy**, **efficiency** and **effectiveness**. 'Economy' refers to prioritising those methods that are most suited to obtaining the best possible results for the resources utilised. The 'holy grail' of efficiency entails the securing of the maximum output of the organisation for the minimum resources expended. 'Effectiveness' refers to the compliance between organisational goals and the actual outputs.*

NMP has been criticised on the following grounds.

- It simply measures outputs, rather than meets social objectives, specific outcomes or human needs.
- It is rooted in neoliberal political economy, which privileges privatisation and competition. Rather than inspire an increase in service levels, such an emphasis may, in fact, be divisive and reduce the quality of services.
- It provides the capitalist state with a new cloak of legitimacy, because blame for failure is now attributed to the service provider and not to the functioning of the state itself.

Benchmarking: measuring and improving performance

The Prison Service has 'Quarterly Performance Ratings' that are published in May, August, November and February of each year. Ratings are based on the following criteria.

1. Cost performance and output data from a weighted scorecard.
2. Compliance with Prison Service standards.
3. Findings from external inspections by HM Chief Inspector of Prisons (HMCIP) and the Independent Monitoring Board (IMB).
4. Views of Prison Service area managers and the Prison Service management board.

The Prison Service is constantly updating its data on penal performance on its website. This can be a source of more up-to-date information for your essays than that which is cited in textbooks.

Key performance indicators 2005 (for public sector prisons)

1. To ensure no escapes of Category A prisoners.
2. To ensure that the number of escapes from prisons and from escorts undertaken by Prison Service staff, expressed as a proportion of the average prison population, is lower than 0.05 per cent.
3. To ensure that the number of escapes from contracted-out escorts is no more than 1 per 20,000 prisoners handled.

(Continued)

4. To ensure that the number of serious assaults, expressed as a proportion of the average prison population, does not exceed the level
   recorded in 2003–04.

5. To ensure that the rate of self-inflicted deaths in 2004–05 does not
   exceed 112.8 per 100,000 of the prison population.

6. To ensure that the average rate of positive results from random
   mandatory drug tests is lower than 10 per cent by April 2005.

7. To ensure that the number of minority ethnic staff in the Prison
   Service is at least 6.0 per cent by April 2005.

8. To improve the proportion of prisoners escorted within the contractor
   area that arrive at court before the court sitting time. Contractor targets:

   - Area 1 75%
   - Area 2 85%
   - Area 3 75%
   - Area 4 75%
   - Area 5 91%
   - Area 6 85%
   - Area 7 80%
   - Area 8 85%

9. To deliver 10,490 accredited offending behaviour programme comple-
   tions in 2004–05, including 1,100 sex offender treatment programmes
   and 3,900 drug programmes.

10. To ensure that the percentage of the prison population that is above
    the uncrowded capacity, expressed as a percentage of the average
    population, does not exceed 24 per cent.

11. Prisoners to achieve:

    - 52,260 basic skills awards, of which 15,870 are at entry level,
      21,890 are at Level 1 and 14,500 are at Level 2;
    - 113,010 key skills awards.

12. To ensure that 34,890 prisoners have a job training or educational out-
    come on release in 2004–05.

13. To ensure that average staff sickness in 2004–05 does not exceed
    12.5 working days per person.

(HM Prison Service, 2005)

Privatisation occurs when government functions are systematically
transferred to the private sector. Cavadino and Dignan (2007) argue

that there are three main ways in which privatisation has impacted on prisons:

- the delivery of services (escorts, employment, catering and education);
- the financing and building of new prisons;
- the management of existing prisons.

The main penal entrepreneurs are: Group 4; Premier Prisons; UKDS; and Tarmac Constructions Ltd. Wolds Remand Centre, run by Group 4, opened in April 1992. There are currently 13 private prisons in England and Wales. Prison privatisation has a very long history, but it was reintroduced in the 1990s because of the:

- penal system being confronted with a number of interrelated crises;
- ideological commitment of New Right to denationalisation;
- belief that privatisation and better management might solve the prisons' crises.

Penal privatisation has been heavily criticised on moral and political grounds.

1.   It is immoral to make profits out of the pain of others.
2.   Labour in private (and public) prisons is a form of penal slavery.
3.   With the increased focus on efficiency, human needs are erased.
4.   It creates tensions and conflict between public and private sectors.
5.   Market testing leads to increasing staff insecurities that may be taken out on prisoners.
6.   Private prisons are less accountable than those in the public sector.
7.   Profits can only be made by having either fewer, and poorly trained, staff or by providing inferior services.
8.   Private prisons are considered to have poor safety records.
9.   The lessons from the USA show us that, in the long run, prison conditions and prisoners' lived experiences are worse, not better, under private regimes.
10. The profit motive drives greater pressure for penal expansion or for keeping people in prison for longer.

Rather than adding to penal legitimacy, privatisation creates new problems in addition to the current crises that the penal system faces.

Common pitfall   *The debate on penal privatisation is polarised. Ensure that you read sources from all of the different perspectives.*

'Making punishment work'

In recent times, there have been three main periods of penal policy. From the late 1980s until 1993, prisons were generally considered to be ineffective and counterproductive. The Home Office White Paper *Crime, Justice and Protecting the Public* (1990) described incarceration as an *'expensive way of making bad people worse'* (p. 6). The government was committed to penal reduction and the Criminal Justice Act 1991 enshrined the principles of just deserts: that punishment should be restricted to serious (i.e. violent and sexual) offences and that the sentence should be proportionate to the offence committed. Much of the success in containing, and then reducing, the prison populations has been attributed to Douglas Hurd, Home Secretary during the late 1980s. From 1993–1997, however, the political landscape changed and Michael Howard, the Conservative Home Secretary during this period, argued that prisons 'worked' in terms of incapacitation and deterrence. The Home Office *Protecting the Public* (1996) stated simply that *'the Government firmly believes that prison works'* (p. 4). Howard advocated increased security, austere regimes and a return to less eligibility.

> **Common pitfall** *There are a number of Criminal Justice Acts and laws relating to prisons, probation and sentencing. Ensure that you always check for recent changes to legislation and government White Papers.*

With the election of 'New' Labour in 1997 came another shift in emphasis. The intention now was to *make* prisons work, with prisons perceived to be a major opportunity to responsibilise and rehabilitate offenders. In 1997, Jack Straw, the first New Labour Home Secretary, made a commitment to constructive regimes, stating *'we believe prisons can be made to work as one element in a radical and coherent strategy to protect the public by reducing crime'* (cited in HMCIP, 1998, p. 19). A little later, influential liberal penal reformer Lord Justice Woolf (2002) argued that '[al]*though prison remains very expensive ... I now believe that it can be an expensive way of making people better'* (p. 6).

New penal credo

Alison Liebling (2004) argued that we have seen the emergence of a *'new penal credo'* (p. 35). This is centred around the following:

(Continued)

- protection of public as key ideology;
- links with other agencies to maximise effectiveness;
- best value from resources;
- standards for all aspects of work;
- regimes and programmes subject to accreditation;
- reducing reoffending as the key outcome.

The most significant policy document on prisons under the New Labour Government is the Halliday Report, *Making Punishments Work* (2001). The Report called for the virtual abolition of short-term sentences and the end to the proportionality principle that underscored the Criminal Justice Act 1991.

*Halliday argued that, instead, sentences should reflect previous convictions. This focus was underscored by the unsubstantiated claim that 50 per cent of all 'crimes' were committed by a hard core of 100,000 persistent offenders. This **persistence principle** for sentencing, however, is only likely to criminalise poor and petty property offenders, and to lead to greater discrimination in the penal system.*

Halliday advocated that intensive efforts should be made to rehabilitate persistent offenders through *'intrusive and punitive sentences'*. The opportunity to protect the public through reducing reoffending would be pursued within an *'appropriate punitive envelope'*. He proposed a twin-track approach in penal policy, distinguishing between tough measures for serious and dangerous offenders, and lenient approaches for ordinary offenders. This bifurcated approach revisited the debates on policy of the 1970s and 1980s (see, for example, Bottoms, 1977; Hudson, 1993). Halliday also proposed a new generic *'community punishment order'* and the need for improved co-operation between criminal justice agencies. The government accepted these proposals in the 2002 White Paper *Justice for All* and the subsequent Criminal Justice Act 2003.

Criminal Justice Act 2003

- Diverts very low-risk offenders out of the court system and punishes them in the community.
- Provides for income-related fines for low-risk offenders.

(Continued)

- Demands community sentences for medium-risk offenders.
- Establishes greater control and surveillance (including satellite tracking) of persistent offenders, combined with help to reduce reoffending.
- Under *Custody plus*, offenders are sentenced to a short spell in prison, followed by a longer period of supervision in the community.
- Under *Custody minus*, offenders who fail to undertake a community punishment are imprisoned.

The fulfilment of the changes brought about by the Halliday Report and the Criminal Justice Act 2003 required major organisational changes in the national probation and prison services. The government duly published the Carter Review, *Managing Offenders, Reducing Crime: A New Approach*, on 6 January 2004. Carter promoted rehabilitation through accredited 'What Works' programmes and argued that, for this to be effective, the 'silos' between the 'correctional' services had to be broken down. This was to be done by creating an umbrella organisation that could provide the case management of offenders from sentence to release. Without consultation, the government published *Reducing Crime, Changing Lives: The Government's Plans for Transforming the Management of Offenders,* which outlined the introduction of a National Offender Management Service (NOMS) in June 2004.

The National Offender Management Service (NOMS)

NOMS bridged the gap between public and private sectors, and between prisons and probation. New regional offender managers (ROMS) owned offender sentence plans and commissioned services, including rehabilitation, from the various providers in the market. This principle of 'contestability', in effect, privatised the rehabilitation of offenders. NOMS is rooted in the principles that better management and interagency co-operation will lead to the greater responsibilisation of offenders; it also adheres to the belief that prison is a 'special place' in which we can both punish and rehabilitate serious criminals. NOMS has been heavily criticised. One undisclosed informant told The Guardian 'it's like putting a goat in charge of an orchard' (23 June 2005), while one senior Home Office civil servant suggested that NOMS might really stand for 'Nightmare on Marsham Street' (ibid.).

A further theme that has developed is that it is the *victim* who is the real customer of the correctional services (Home Office, 2004c). The government wishes to bring about a cultural change to improve customer services and to reduce offending in the interests of victims. According to Tony Blair (2004):

> Sentencing will ensure the public is protected from the most dangerous and hardened criminals but will offer the rest the chance of rehabilitation ... This whole programme amounts to a modernising and rebalancing of the entire criminal justice system in favour of victims and the community.

Penal pressure groups often provide invaluable commentaries on recent policies.

Cognitive behaviouralism and what works

Under New Labour, properly managed prisons are seen as an opportunity to responsibilise offenders and to reduce the risk of reoffending. A sentence of imprisonment is expected to transform serious and persistent offenders by improving their life skills and addressing the drivers that can trigger crime. Prisoners should be given opportunities to make choices that help them to learn how to behave responsibly. This responsibilisation process is managed and integrated with other criminal justice agencies and punishments in the community. Reducing the risk of reoffending is tied to the 'What Works' rehabilitative agenda, which roots the causes of offending behaviour in each individual offender's cognitive defects and deficient thinking skills. There are a number of accredited 'What Works' programmes in prison.

'What Works'

- Reasoning and rehabilitation (R&R)
- Enhanced thinking skills (ETS)
- Making offenders rethink everything (MORE)
- Controlling anger and learning to manage it (CALM)
- Cognitive self-change programme (CSCP)
- Sex offender treatment programmes (SOTPs, of which there are six)

Critics have claimed, however, that the 'What Works' rehabilitative programmes are epistemologically flawed. This is because 'What Works':

- individualises and pathologises offenders;
- 'others' prisoners as cognitively different;
- demands choice, agency and acting responsibly, all of which, in the prison setting, are virtually non-existent;
- privileges rehabilitation so that, if it fails or is rejected, it is the individual's fault because of his or her own inadequacies;
- leads to further individualisation or redefinition as 'dangerousness' and therefore untreatable;
- focuses on self-governance, and ignores wider social contexts and divisions (such as poverty), doing nothing to change such problematic social circumstances;
- treatment remains within a punitive framework of security, control and punishment;
- predicates and justifies improved conditions on reducing offending;
- adds penal legitimacy through the humane cloak of rehabilitation.

Common pitfall   *Do not confuse 'What Works' with 'prison works'. Both ideologies argue that prison has a utility, but each focuses on very different philosophical justifications.*

Decency, moral performance and human rights

Managerialism has become all-pervasive in penal policy during the last two decades. Humanitarian penologists and practitioners have looked to counter the dehumanising aspects of managerialism in three ways:

- promoting decency;
- promoting moral performance;
- promoting human rights.

The 'decency' agenda was initiated by Martin Narey (HM Prison Service Director General, 1999–2003) and his successor Phil Wheatley.

> The decency agenda is intended to run like a golden thread through all aspects of the service's work. Decency means treatment within the law, delivering promised standards, providing fit and proper facilities, giving prompt attention to prisoners concerns and protecting them from harm. It means providing prisoners with a regime that gives variety and helps them to rehabilitate. It means fair and consistent treatment by staff.

(HM Prison Service, 2003a, p. 29)

Decency

Decency would appear to relate to the following.

- *Physical conditions* Decent living conditions, cleanliness, access to showers, and a safe, decent and healthy environment.
- *Staff-prisoner relationships* Officers treating prisoners as they would treat a family member or as they would like to be treated themselves; developing positive relationships; that prisoners should be treated with dignity and respect; use of language (i.e. serving meals, not 'feeding time') and calling prisoners by their first names.
- *Legality* Prisons are lawful and fair, and prisoners receive their legal entitlements.
- *Anything questioning legitimacy* Acknowledging institutional racism, prison officer brutality and responding to horrendous suicide rates.

The problems with the decency agenda are:

- it has no clear definition—'*it means all things to all people*';
- it is nothing new—'*old wine in new bottles*';
- it is not focused on the experiences of prisoners;
- it benefits from no powers of enforcement;
- it re-legitimises prison.

The evaluative criteria of 'moral performance' are championed by liberal penologist Alison Liebling. She argues that there have been many positive changes in imprisonment following the rise of performance indicators. Liebling argues that this managerialist agenda can be expanded by undertaking appreciative inquiries (AI) into prison life and by developing 'Measuring Quality of Prison Life' (MQPL) surveys.

Moral performance

Alison Liebling (2004, pp. 154–5) identifies '*what matters*' in the moral performance of prisons as follows:

- *Relationship dimensions* Respect; humanity; relationships; trust; support.
- *Regime dimensions* Fairness; order; safety; well-being; personal development; family contact; decency.

(Continued)

- *Social structure dimensions* Power; social life.
- *Individual items* Meaning; quality of life.

The idea of moral performance has, however, been criticised on the following grounds:

- the limits of the AI methodology;
- it is predicated on managerialism;
- it benefits from no legal compulsion;
- it works on the terrain of state discourses;
- it fails to connect with broader structural/socio-economic contexts;
- it re-legitimates prisons;
- prisons are profoundly immoral places.

A third response has been to promote prisoners' human rights. This gained some momentum with the implementation of the Human Rights Act 1998 (HRA) in October 2000, but the courts have interpreted the HRA conservatively, while the Prison Service has largely ignored it and has given staff little training. When the HRA has been discussed in official documents, the Service has outlined how it believes current policies are '*ECHR* [European Convention on Human Rights]-*proof*', vigorously defended them, or emphasised the importance of responsibilities.

> The Government's objective is to promote a culture of rights and responsibilities throughout our society. The Act will make people *more aware of the rights they already have* but also balance these with responsibilities to others.
>
> (HM Prison Service, 2000, p. 1, emphasis added)

The promotion of human rights remains an underdeveloped response to managerial forms of penal performance.

Resettlement and pathways out of crime

The Social Exclusion Report (Social Exclusion Unit, 2002) identified a number of key factors involved in reoffending. These included truancy, unemployment, illicit substance misuse, health, debt, homelessness, social capital and family problems.

Offender Pathways

The Home Office's Reducing Reoffending: National Action Plan (2004b) identified a number of 'Pathways' out of crime, relating to the following factors.

- Pathway 1 Accommodation
- Pathway 2 Education, training and employment
- Pathway 3 Mental and physical health
- Pathway 4 Drugs and alcohol
- Pathway 5 Finance, benefit and debt
- Pathway 6 Children and the families of offenders
- Pathway 7 Attitudes, thinking and behaviour

Part of the role of the Prison Service is to help to resettle offenders back into the community on release. Despite the many different problems identified as confronting prisoner 'resettlement', the Service has, to date, only been actively involved in assisting ex-prisoners and those on parole to find employment and/or accommodation.

In recent times, prison industries and workshops have aimed to provide skills that fit the demands of the labour market. This draws remarkable parallels with the arguments proposed by Marxist penologists.

"Is the Prison Service committed to treating prisoners with dignity and respect?"

You need to consider the main Prison Service statements on dignity and respect. This will include a discussion of 'decency', the aims of the Service and its statement of purpose, and other policy initiatives, such as those focusing on race relations. You should also consider the manner in which the Prison Service has defined prisoner human rights.

Taking it **FURTHER**

Are we witnessing the emergence of 'welfare through punishment'?

Effectively managed prisons are presented as a major opportunity for reducing the likelihood of reoffending and for 'bringing home' prisoners' responsibilities. Without rejecting the goals of deterrence and incapacitation, rehabilitation is tied into wider utilitarian goals of crime reduction and is advocated as one of the primary ends of imprisonment. The welfare role of imprisonment, however, takes on new significance, because it operates within a context of a declining commitment to social insurance, and a greater push towards the criminalisation and penalisation of the powerless. The doctrine of 'welfare *through* punishment' promises to protect legitimate consumers (i.e. victims) by facilitating the re-entry into the labour market of responsibilised offenders. The prison is conceived as a new workhouse, in which the non-productive sub-proletariat can be trained to be a potentially valuable commodity—i.e. given the skills, discipline and work ethic needed for employment. We must consider whether this means that we are confronted with the horrible spectre of prisons and their correctional partners operating as a buffer system between the poor and welfare support. Rather than responding to need, welfare priorities are restricted for those at society's extremities only once they have been criminalised and already embroiled in the process of penalisation.

The limitations of welfare *through* punishment are immediately apparent. Procedural rights of the accused are virtually irrelevant. Notions of 'justice' are reduced to improved conviction rates and reduced costs. Any sense of a prisoner's entitlement, rights, conditions or claims to humanity are intimately tied to his or her ability, or potential, to provide a productive form of labour in a capitalist economy within which demand outstrips supply. The individual human suffering of prisoners and its acknowledgement are inconsequential to wider utilitarian aims. A reversal of fortune, it can be assumed, may lead to a return of its sister doctrine, less eligibility. Worryingly, the contraction of welfare provision may mean that, in times of economic decline, political pressure may mount for a long-term suppression of prisoner welfare rights. Yet it is clear that those in need of welfare should always be conceived of *beyond* punishment.

Textbook guide

CAVADINO, M AND DIGNAN, J **(2007)** *The Penal System*, 4th edn, London: Sage
CLARKE, J AND NEWMAN, J **(1997)** *The Managerial State*, London: Sage

FITZGERALD, M AND SIM, J **(1982)** *British Prisons*, 2nd edn, Oxford: Blackwell

JEWKES, Y (ED) **(2007A)** *Handbook of Prisons*, Cullompton: Willan Publishing

LIEBLING, A **(2004)** *Prisons and their Moral Performance*, Oxford: Oxford University Press

RYAN, M **(2005)** *Penal Policy and Political Culture*, Winchester: Waterside Press

RYAN, M AND WARD, T **(1989)** *Privatization and the Penal System*, Milton Keynes: Open University Press

2.7

penal administration and prisoner populations

Core areas: **the structure of the penal administration in England and Wales**

the penal estate

current prison populations

locking up the dangerous or punishing the poor?

prisons in Northern Ireland and Scotland

Running themes

- Human rights
- Legitimacy
- Less eligibility
- Managerialism
- Pains of imprisonment
- Power to punish
- Public protection
- Social divisions

The structure of the penal administration in England and Wales

On 9 May 2007, responsibility for prisons, probation and sentencing was moved from the Home Office to the Department of Constitutional Affairs, which was renamed the Ministry of Justice. Lord Falconer of Thoroton was originally appointed as the new Secretary of Justice, but, at the end of June 2007, Gordon Brown, the new Prime Minister, replaced Lord Falconer with Jack Straw.

The core components of the new Ministry of Justice

- The National Offender Management Service—an umbrella organisation that provides the administration of correctional services in England and Wales through HM Prison Service and the National Probation Service (NPS).
- The Youth Justice Board.
- The Parole Board, HM Inspectorates of Prison and Probation, IMBs, and the Prison and Probation Ombudsman.
- The Sentencing Guidelines Council.
- The Office for Criminal Justice Reform.
- HM Courts Service—administration of the civil, family and criminal courts in England and Wales.

The National Offender Management Service (NOMS) deals with the delivery of prison and probation services. The nine ROMs in England, and the Director of Offender Management in Wales, commission offender services from a range of providers in the public and private sectors. The current Chief Executive of NOMS is Helen Edwards and she chairs the NOMS board, which includes the Director General of HM Prison Service and the Director of Probation. NOMS has a budget of around £4 billion. The aims of NOMS are to:

- protect the public;
- reduce reoffending;
- punish offenders;
- rehabilitate offenders;
- ensure that victims feel that justice has been done.

The current Director General of HM Prison Service is Phil Wheatley. Since 1993, the Prison Service has been an executive agency of the

Home Office (now Ministry of Justice). The HM Prison Service 'statement of purpose' reads:

> Her Majesty's Prison Service serves the public by keeping in custody those committed by the courts. Our duty is to look after them with humanity and help them lead law-abiding and useful lives in custody and after release.

> (www.hmprisonservice.gov.uk)

The Home Office was the main government body for penal administration before May 2007. It continues to exist, but is now more focused on security.

Since June 2004, the Prison Service has been part of NOMS. Sixty-eight per cent of NOMS' 70,000 staff work within the Prison Service branch.

The main aims and priorities of HM Prison Service for 2005–06

- Ensuring safe and decent conditions for prisoners
- Reducing reoffending and improving prisoners' prospects on release
- Maintaining order and control
- Increasing diversity and equality
- Maintaining security and preventing escapes
- Improving health care

The penal estate

In 2007, there were 139 prisons (126 public and 13 private) in England and Wales. The budget for HM Prison Service is £2.6 billion per annum. It costs £600 per week on average for each prisoner (i.e. £30,000+ per annum). There are a number of different categories of prisons and prisoners for adult male prisoners.

Types of prison

1. Open prisons
2. Closed prisons:

   - local;
   - training;
   - high security ('dispersal prisons').

Not all prisoners have been convicted or sentenced. Remand prisoners make up around 19 per cent of the total prison population and the average length of time spent on remand is two months. It is worth noting that many people on remand do not receive custodial sentences at trial. There are also a small number of civil prisoners. These are people who have not broken the criminal law, but who have breached procedural rules such as 'contempt of court'.

Who works in prisons?

The officers of a prison, as stipulated under the Prison Act 1952, are:

- prison governor (grades 1–5 and governing governor who set budgets);
- prison medical officers (doctors, nurses, medical officers, mental health specialists);
- prison chaplains.

Other members of staff that you will find in a prison include:

- prison officers (basic/senior/principal);
- suicide awareness coordinator;
- probation officers (seconded to the prison for five years);
- psychologists;
- educational (teachers);
- resettlement;
- counselling, assessment, referral, advice and throughcare (CARAT) workers;
- instructors (works unit, physical instructors, farms);
- operational grade support (work on the gate);
- administration (civil servants).

Current prison populations

In September 2005, Charles Clarke, then Home Secretary, announced that the government had abandoned its target of keeping the upper limits of the prison population at around 80,000. According to recent Home Office estimates, the ADP for prisoners in 2010 will be at least 91,000. The current prison population reached a new high of 80,000 in December 2006, but then declined. By early 2007, however, it had once again breached 80,000. Between June 2006 and June 2007, the average daily population of prisoners increased by 3,019 (see Tables 2.2 and 2.3).

Table 2.2 Prisoner population in England and Wales on 1 June 2007

Male	75,973
Female	4,377
Number of prisoners held in police cells under Operation Safeguard	264
TOTAL	**80,614**
Useable operational capacity	**81,058**
Spaces available under Operation Safeguard*	**400**
TOTAL	**81,458**
Number under Home Detention Curfew supervision	**2,269**

*These vary from night to night and up to a 400-place ceiling.

Table 2.3 Prisoner population in England and Wales on 1 June 2006

Male	73,139
Female	4,456
Number of prisoners held in police cells under Operation Safeguard	0
TOTAL	**77,595**
Useable operational capacity	**79,498**
Number under Home Detention Curfew supervision	**2,804**

Prison data snapshots

The following three dates and sets of ADP prisoner figures are worth remembering.

- December 1992 40,600 prisoners—*the lowest recorded rate of ADP of prisoners in recent times.*
- May 1997 60,131 prisoners—*the ADP of prisoners when the New Labour government was elected.*
- June 2007 81,007 prisoners—*the ADP of prisoners during the week in which Gordon Brown became Prime Minister.*

At any one time, approximately 40 per cent of prisoners have been convicted of offences related to fraud, theft, burglary or robbery. About 15 per cent of prisoners are convicted of drug offences, which are often linked to property offences; 15 per cent of convictions are related to sexual offences and 20 per cent are for violent offences (see Figure 2.2). Approximately 80 per cent of convicted and sentenced prisoners are released within one year.

Common pitfall *Examining the average daily population (ADP) alone can give you a distorted perception. Statistics are socially constructed. The number of people in various different forms of custody in the United Kingdom is much higher than 80,000 and is likely soon to break through the 100,000 mark.*

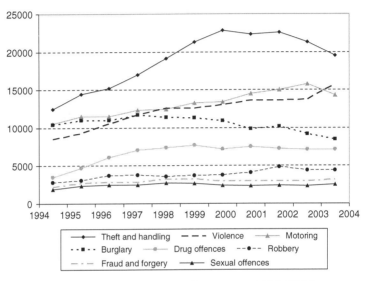

Figure 2.2   Receptions into prison by offence type 1994–2004
Source: Newburn (2007)

The exorbitant rise in prison populations is a political and policy choice, and is not a response to the official 'crime' rate. Indeed, the official 'crime' rate has declined.

According to the official 'crime' statistics and the British Crime Survey (BCS), most 'crimes' are actually going down.

British Crime Survey (BCS) figures have been on a downward trend since 1995, after a long upward trend since 1981. Police-recorded figures from the period between 1991 and 1997 identified a downward trend, but these figures have been much more ambiguous in the last ten years. In July 2006, the BCS estimated that the total 'crime' against private households amounted to 10.9 million offences annually. This compares with an estimated 16.7 million offences annually in 1999: a fall of 35 per cent.

Home Office estimates of offences: custody ratio (1999)

- *Offences reported 45.2% (of all offences committed)*
- *Offences recorded 24.3%*
- *Offences leading to caution or conviction 3.0%*
- *Offences leading to conviction 2.2%*
- *Offences leading to custody 0.3%*

This is limited data, but, given that practitioners and politicians often present such figures as accurate and reliable accounts, their decline at the same time as prison populations increase is significant.

There are a number of reasons why the prison population has increased, including:

- *longer prison sentences;*
- *increasing custody rates;*
- *more people on remand;*
- *the use of indeterminate sentences;*
- *the collapse of the fine;*
- *the reduced use of the Home Detention Curfew;*
- *increasing risk aversion on behalf of parole boards;*
- *more recalls of people for breaches of community sentences;*
- *the external pressures of a law and order society that uses punitive rhetoric to exploit people's fears and anxieties to gain political ascendancy;*
- *internal pressures and the needs of professionals.*

Recidivism rates for ex-prisoners remain high. The Home Office (2003) estimated that 75 per cent of young offenders and 50 per cent of adult offenders reoffended within two years of release.

Locking up the dangerous or punishing the poor?

Although we often hear arguments that we punish the dangerous and protect the public, when we look at the facts of who is imprisoned and their social backgrounds, a different picture begins to emerge.

Prison data

- *Sentences* 81% of prison population convicted
- *Men* 92% of prison population
- *Women* 8% of prison population
- *Age* 23% under the age of 21 and 52% under the age of 30
- *Class* 83% of male prisoners are working class
- *Black* 19% men and 25% women

Prisoners are more likely to be socially deprived and harmed individuals than seriously dangerous to society.

Social backgrounds of prison populations

1. Have been in care or have family difficulties:

   - 27% in care as child;
   - two-and-a-half times as likely to have had a family member convicted of a criminal offence.

2. Are unemployed or on benefits:

   - 5% of general population unemployed, but 67% of prisoners have been unemployed during the four weeks before imprisonment;
   - 13.7% of working-age population are in receipt of benefits, but 72% have been in receipt of benefits immediately before entry to prison;
   - 75% of prisoners do not have paid employment to go to on release.

3. Homeless:

   - 1 in 14 prisoners are homeless at the time of imprisonment;
   - 32% of prisoners are not living in permanent accommodation prior to imprisonment.

4. No education:

   - 80% have writing skills, 65% have numeracy skills and 50% have reading skills at, or below, the level of an 11-year-old child;
   - 52% of male and 71% of female adult prisoners have no qualifications at all.

(Continued)

5. In poor health:

- 80% of prisoners have mental health problems;
- 46% of sentenced adult male prisoners aged 18–49 reported having a long-standing illness or disability;
- 15 times as likely to be HIV positive;
- 60–70% of prisoners were using drugs before imprisonment.

(Social Exclusion Unit, 2002)

Young people in custody

Those children who are criminalised and penalised are generally from vulnerable backgrounds. Rather than presenting a threat to adults, children in secure custody have, more often than not, been harmed by adults. Many children in custody have experienced difficult family relationships, impoverished social backgrounds and have difficulties in coping with the problems with which they are confronted in life. To add to these problems, they are taken away from what is familiar to them and placed in an unfriendly, stigmatising and physically austere environment, which may be overcrowded and which is rooted in conflict, power struggles and bullying. For penal commentators such as Barry Goldson and Debs Coles, such a deliberately painful state of affairs has, quite rightly, been described as *'institutional child abuse'* and these critics have called for its abolition.

Children and young people in custody or secure accommodation

Social backgrounds

- *Involved in care or social services 50%*
- *Mental health issues 85%*
- *Serious drug addictions (e.g. heroin) 14%*
- *Alcohol problems 66%*
- *Victim of violence at home 25%*
- *Victim of sexual abuse (girls) 33%*
- *Victim of sexual abuse (boys) 5%*

(Continued)

Custodial institutions

- 3250 places for young people
- 17 Young Offender Institutions (YOIs)
- 26 Local Authority Secure Children's Homes (LASCHs)
- 4 Secure Training Centres

Plus

- Remands in adult prisons
- Children in care homes

Black and minority ethnic prisoners

The problem of racism is deeply rooted in the history of the Prison Service. In the 1970s, many officers were members of the overtly racist organisation, the National Front.

There is evidence of extreme racism among prison officers, and of the brutal treatment and harassment of minority ethnic prisoners. In 1999, Martin Narey, then its Director General, admitted that the Prison Service was 'institutionally racist'.

Many prison staff have been accused of overreacting to disruptive behaviour by Black prisoners and of falsely stereotyping them as 'big, Black and dangerous'. There have also been dubious statements about Black victims in prison. In 1998, Richard Tilt, former Director General, made the unsubstantiated claim that Black prisoners were more likely to die from positional asphyxia while being restrained because of their genetic disposition to sickle cell anaemia.

Black/minority ethnic prisoner populations

- In 1985, there were 8 per cent (men) and 12 per cent (women) from Black or minority ethnic (ME) groups. (See current data above).
- There were 26,043 prisoners from ME groups received into public sector prisons in England and Wales during the year Apr 2004–Mar 2005.
- Of all first receptions recorded under the 2001 Census codes, 78 per cent were White, 12 per cent were Black or Black British, 6 per cent Asian or

---

(Continued)

Asian British, 3 per cent were of mixed ethnicity and 1 per cent of other ethnic groups.
- Between 1993 and 2003, White and Asian prison population increased by 48 per cent and 73 per cent, respectively. The Black and ME prisoner population increased by 138 per cent.
- In 2003, 37 per cent of Black and ME prisoners were foreign nationals.

The death of Zahid Mubarek at Feltham YOI in March 2000 led to a number of official inquiries. The Commission for Racial Equality published two reports in 2003, which led to the HM Prison Service Prison Service Action Plan on race relations (2003b). The HMCIP published its thematic study Parallel Lives in 2005, while in 2006, the Keith Inquiry published its two-volume Report of the Zahid Mubarek Inquiry.

In February 2003, of those whose nationality was known, 12 per cent of the male prison population and 21 per cent of all women prisoners were foreign nationals. In 2007, there were believed to be over 10,000 foreign national prisoners in England and Wales. Foreign national prisoners are confronted with a variety of problems, concerns and socio-economic disadvantages, not least of which are the language barriers. The prospect of deportation and revocation of their immigration status may also increase anxiety, uncertainty and the pains of imprisonment. There is evidence in HM Inspectorate of Prisons' reports of racism, and of the use of inappropriate language and comments. For critics, imprisonment, detention and immigration policies must be understood within the context of state racism. This analysis considers how *'institutional racism and popular racism are woven into state racism'* (Sivanandan, 2001, p. 3).

Official data can evidence social problems and social divisions.

Women in prison

The experiences and differential pains of imprisonment for women have largely been ignored.

Women prisoners

Populations

- *1965*   841
- *1992*   1,353
- *1999*   3,400
- *2004*   4,672
- *2007*   4,368

Social backgrounds

- *Unemployed 66%*
- *Non-violent crimes 72%*
- *Drugs/substance misuse 66%*
- *Care and abuse 40%*
- *Mothers 40%*
- *Black 25%*
- *Attempted suicide before prison 10%*

Prisons

In 2007, there were 19 prisons for women (including with-male prisons or remand centres).

Recidivism rates

65 per cent of ex-prisoners reoffend within two years.

Women offenders have been more likely to be understood through positivistic psychobiological theories of crime and to be responded to more as psychiatric patients than as offenders.

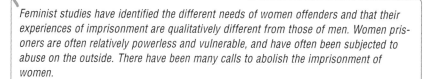

Feminist studies have identified the different needs of women offenders and that their experiences of imprisonment are qualitatively different from those of men. Women prisoners are often relatively powerless and vulnerable, and have often been subjected to abuse on the outside. There have been many calls to abolish the imprisonment of women.

Prisons in Northern Ireland and Scotland

Northern Ireland Prison Service (NIPS) is an executive agency of the Northern Ireland Office (NIO), established on 1 April 1995. Its main statutory duties are detailed in the Prison Act (Northern Ireland) 1953. Prison rules, providing guidance for the operation of the Prison Service, are made under the Act. The current Director General of the NIPS is Robin Masefield.

Prisons in Northern Ireland

The NIPS currently has three operational establishments:

- HMP Maghaberry;
- HMP Magilligan;
- HMP Prison and Young Offenders Centre Hydebank.

In the 1970s–1990s, the NIPS was heavily criticised for its treatment of political prisoners. A number of notorious prisons, such as the Maze, have been closed since the peace settlement in the 1990s. The current NIPS 'statement of purpose' reads:

> The Northern Ireland Prison Service, through our staff, serves the community by keeping in secure, safe and humane custody those committed by the courts; by working with prisoners and with organisations, seeks to reduce the risk of re-offending; and in so doing aims to protect the public and to contribute to peace and stability in Northern Ireland.

> (www.niprisonservice.gov.uk)

The NIPS has traditionally had low prison populations. In 1920, there were only 278 people in prison (Tomlinson, 1996). There was, however, a major escalation from the late 1960s, when the prison population rose from below 700 (of which 9 were women) to a peak of 3,000 in 1979. Since then, the population (sentenced and remand) has steadily fallen to around 1,400 prisoners. The total prison population on the 19 December 2005, for example, was 1308 (see Table 2.4). The figures included 30 women prisoners and 9 immigration detainees. On the 20 December 2006, the population stood at 1,425 prisoners, including 32 women and 1 immigration detainee. More recently, on the 10 September 2007, there were 1,444 sentenced and remand prisoners in Northern Ireland, 49 of whom were women, alongside 4 immigration detainees.

The NIPS employs around 2,000 staff in a wide variety of posts. Of these, 1,600 are uniformed staff, 10 are teachers, 66 are hospital or nursing staff, and 28 are physical education instructors. There has been a

Table 2.4   Population details for prisons in Northern Ireland on 19 December 2005

Establishments	Sentenced	Remand	Immigration detainees	Total
Maghaberry	348	346	4	698
Magilligan	406	0	0	406
Hydebank Wood (female)	12	13	5	30
Hydebank Wood (male)	86	88	0	174
Total	852	447	9	1308

very large fall in prison officer numbers since 1998: a reduction of around 40 per cent.

The Scottish Prison Service (SPS) is an agency of the Scottish Executive and the current Chief Executive of the SPS board is Tony Cameron. The SPS has a budget of more than £320 million and employs over 15,000 members of staff. There are currently 15 penal establishments in Scotland.

Table 2.5   SPS prisoner population on Friday 9 March 2007

Untried male adults	1,110
Untried female adults	61
Untried male young offenders	300
Untried female young offenders	14
Sentenced male adults	4,619
Sentenced female adults	204
Sentenced male young offenders	622
Sentenced female young offenders	31
Recalled life prisoners	68
Convicted prisoners awaiting sentencing	208
Prisoners awaiting deportation	8
All Scotland Total	**7,245**

SPS key activities

The SPS' *Annual Report* (2006) highlights that its key activities for 2006–07 will include:

- ending slopping out in HM YOI Polmont in 2007;
- working on ways forward for Peterhead prison;
- creating seven new, or completely rebuilt, prisons in the decade from 1999;

(Continued)

- introducing integrated case management for all newly sentenced offenders;
- implementing Home Detention Curfew (HDC);
- working in partnership with community justice authorities (CJAs), and with private and voluntary sector partners;
- beginning construction at HMP Addiewell;
- awarding a contract for a new prison at Bishopbriggs.

"What is the current organisational structure of the Prison Service in England and Wales?"

To answer this question, you will need to look at the Ministry of Justice, National Offender Management Service and HM Prison Service. You will need to understand how these three bodies interrelate, which will probably require you to look up recent data on the Internet. A good student will be able to tell the examiner what is happening at the time they are writing. Do not be complacent and give out-of-date accounts. That little bit of extra work can make all the difference to your marks.

Taking it **FURTHER**

When examining the social backgrounds of prisoners, you may have been surprised or shocked at the findings: prisoners are generally people from harmed social backgrounds who have perpetrated relatively harmless acts. What does this tell us about the current role of imprisonment and how might this impact upon its political legitimacy?

Textbook guide

BOWLING, B AND PHILLIPS, C (2002) *Racism, Crime and Justice*, London: Longman

BRYANS, S AND JONES, R (EDS) (2001) *Prisons and the Prisoner*, London: HMSO

CARLEN, P AND WORRALL, A (2004) *Analysing Women's Imprisonment*, Cullompton: Willan Publishing

CAVADINO, M AND DIGNAN, J (2007) *The Penal System*, 4th edn, London: Sage

CHIGWADA-BAILEY, R (2003) *Black Women's Experience of Criminal Justice*, Winchester: Waterside Press

COYLE, A (2005) *Understanding Prisons*, Milton Keynes: Open University Press

2.8
sociologies of prison life

Core areas: **sociological studies of imprisonment**
prison conditions
prisoner health

 Running themes

- Human rights
- Legitimacy
- Less eligibility
- Managerialism
- Pains of imprisonment
- Power to punish
- Social divisions

Key penologists

Erving Goffman (1922–82) One of the most influential social thinkers in the twentieth century, Erving Goffman studied sociology and anthropology at the University of Toronto. He undertook his PhD on social interactions in a small island community on the Scottish coast. After studying at Chicago, he spent much of his working life at the University of Pennsylvania. Goffman looked at the mechanics of social interactions and his main writings include *The Presentation of the Self in Everyday Life* (1956) and *Asylums* (1961), his famous analysis of inmates at a Washington mental institution. Goffman died of cancer at the age of 60 in 1982.

James B Jacobs (born 1947) Currently director of the Centre for Research in Crime and Justice at New York University, James B Jacobs was awarded a PhD from Chicago University in 1975. Jacobs is perhaps most well known for his

Weberian study of Stateville penitentiary, Illinois, which was published in 1977. In this study, he presented a historical examination of the total prison organisation, investigating the role of administrators, and the lived realities of prisoners in authoritarian and legal bureaucratic forms of penal authority.

Gresham Sykes (born 1920) A key sociological thinker, Gresham Sykes is Professor Emeritus of Sociology at the University of Virginia, USA. Sykes was born at Plainfield, New Jersey, and served in the US armed forces during World War II. He first came to international prominence through his work with David Matza on the techniques of neutralisation. His most influential penological study is his book *Society of Captives*, first published fifty years ago in 1958 and republished in 2007 with a new epilogue by Sykes.

Sociological studies of imprisonment

The sociologies of prison life have investigated the experiences and lived realities of prisoners and prison staff. They have generally looked at:

- the extent and nature of the pains of imprisonment;
- the different pains of imprisonment of men and women, and how these pains are compounded by disabilities, racism or homophobia;
- whether the prison code is imported into or, created through the deprivations of, prison and/or exported to wider society;
- how prisoners and prison officers develop strategies of psychological survival;
- the structure and transmission of informal rules, 'ways of life', cultures and argots;
- the exercise of penal power (legal and coercive) and the management of prison conflicts;
- order, control and the prevalence of violence in everyday life;
- the nature of penal controversies and the moral legitimacy of imprisonment.

Sociological studies have investigated many different aspects of prison life, with authors often combining a number of the above issues in their work.

The sociologies of prison life remind us of the importance of looking at both the penal environment and the wider social contexts in which imprisonment is situated. There are a number of classic sociological studies of prisons and prisoners. One of the most important early works was Donald Clemmer's *The Prison Community* (1948). This was a study of the maximum-security prison at Menard, Illinois.

> *Clemmer argued that prison subcultures were imported, and reflected the confinement of predominantly male, lower class and poorly educated populations.*

Clemmer also argued that there existed a prisoner code emphasising loyalty, which embodied the norms and values of social backgrounds of prisoners. The code was pro-prisoner and anti-authority, and led to a process of *'prisonisation'*, which provided a means of protecting prisoners.

A slightly later book, but one that laid the foundations for many subsequent studies, was Gresham Sykes' *The Society of Captives* (1958). Sykes was interested in prisoner subcultures and the exercise of power at New Jersey State Maximum Security Prison, Trenton. Sykes argued that the exercise of power by prison officials lacked legitimacy and identified how officers had to offer prisoners rewards to gain their co-operation.

> *Sykes maintained that the prisoner subculture arose as an attempt to mitigate the deprivations that are created by the inherent pains of imprisonment: the deprivation of liberty, goods and services, of heterosexual relationships, and of autonomy and security.*

Sykes also highlighted the ways in which prisoners developed a special language or 'argot', which was a means of communicating with other prisoners.

Erving Goffman's *Asylums* (1963) has also reached classic status. Goffman argued that the *'total institution'*—in his study, a mental hospital—stripped an individual of the social and cultural supports of his or her identity. This led to institutionalisation and a disculturalisation, under which people unlearn their normal social skills and sense of self. An inmate's self was recreated through the daily rituals of institutional life, although this process could be reversed when the inmate returned to his or her previous social setting. Goffman also examined power and status in the total institution. He argued that total institutions were inherently conflictual, leading to antagonistic stereotypes between inmates and supervisors, and pressure on staff to ensure compliance from inmates.

> **Common pitfall** *Remember that, although we can learn many things by studying similar institutions to the prison, there are also many differences between asylums and other 'total institutions'.*

In a very important English study, Stan Cohen and Laurie Taylor undertook research while teaching at the maximum-security wing of Durham Prison. In *Psychological Survival* (first published in 1972), they produced a detailed and disturbing account of how long-term prisoners cope with the psychologically devastating consequences of being deprived of their liberty. For lifers in Durham prison, the self came under serious threat, undermined by a sense of futility that brought into question the meaning of life. But adaptation, passivity and powerlessness were not the only possible outcomes: prisoners could resist. Cohen and Taylor pointed not only to the inherent threats of long-term imprisonment, but also to the importance of resistance within an individual's psychological well-being.

In another well-known study, Israel Barak-Glantz (1981) developed a typology of four models of prison management.

- **'Authoritarian'** In this type, virtually all power is in the hands of the warden.
- **'Bureaucratic-Lawful'** This model is characterised by bureaucratisation, decentralisation, the diffusion of power and the atomisation of the inmate community.
- **'Shared-Powers'** This places a premium on keeping physical controls to a minimum and sees the development of prisoner pressure groups.
- **'Inmate-Control'** Under this model, competing gangs—usually based on ethnic origin—control prisons.

> **Common pitfall** *Some of the earlier sociological studies looked exclusively at the experiences of men and the operation of male prisons. Some of these theories do not always fit easily with the experiences of women.*

In recent times, there have also been a number of sociological studies on prison officers. In *Doing Prison Work* (2004), Elaine Crawley examined the social world of prison officers and their families. Her main focus was on the manner in which prison work is about the management of human emotions. Another influential study is Alison Liebling and David Price's *The Prison Officer* (2001). Liebling and Price undertook an AI into the culture of prison officers and their relationships with prisoners. They argued that prison officers used '*talk*' and other hidden skills to develop positive relationships with prisoners. Underusing their powers, and relying on foresight, diplomacy, humour, discretion and their personal authority, prison officers performed a peacekeeping function.

In contrast to Liebling and Price, David Scott (2006) argued that personal authority is actually deployed to enforce an asymmetrical deference norm and secure prisoner deference. The study identified four working personalities: the careerist; the humanitarian; the mortgage payer; and the disciplinarian—the dominant personality, which was immersed within the principles of less eligibility. Kelsey Kauffman (1988) undertook a detailed study of prison officers at Walpole prison, USA. A former prison officer, Kauffman highlighted the importance of solidarity and loyalty among prison officers, and the development of an informal officer code of conduct. She suggested that prison officer cultures effectively 'other' prisoners as lesser human beings. For Kauffman, that occupational culture is comprised of functionaries—i.e. officers who have emotionally distanced themselves from prisoners.

Read widely and look at the sociological literature from the United Kingdom and the USA. Be prepared to look at journal articles for sociological studies of prison life.

Prison conditions

Prison conditions have been central to the main penological traditions. For those who believe that prisons work through deterrence, prison conditions have been suppressed, because prison life must always be worse than living conditions on the outside. Liberal and humanitarian penologists have consistently called for better conditions for prisoners and have advocated minimum legal standards. Abolitionists have argued that, even if prison conditions were to be vastly improved, it would not necessarily lead to greater penal legitimacy. Prisons with good living conditions are still rooted in the deliberate infliction of pain through the deprivation of liberty.

Prison conditions

Physical conditions inside

- Size of cells
- In-cell furnishings
- Overcrowding and time in cell
- Sanitation
- Clothes
- Showers and personal hygiene
- Food
- Purposeful activity (work and leisure facilities)
- Levels of discipline, control and intimidation

Outside contact

- Letters
- Telephone calls
- Visits
- Media

Overcrowding has been a major problem for the Prison Service in recent years. The overcrowding rate in the 32 male local prisons in 2006 was 53 per cent. There was overcrowding of over 10,000 places and 74 of the 139 penal institutions had populations above their certified normal accommodation, with 15 above operational capacity (i.e. above the safety level). The consequences of overcrowding include:

- negative impact on everything to do with the prison regime, including fewer work and educational facilities;
- 17,000 prisoners are held in pairs in cells that are designed for 1;
- police cells are used to contain prisoners;
- early release of prisoners.

The Howard League provides the most comprehensive and up-to-date information on prison overcrowding.

Prisoner health

The psychological damage that imprisonment inflicts can have a negative impact on the health of all prisoners. Prison is damaging to people, rather than leading to feelings of well-being, support or growth. Three 'hot topics' in relation to prisoners' health are mental health, self-inflicted deaths, and illicit substance misuse and the spread of infectious diseases.

Mental health

The most vulnerable people in prison, as in wider society, are those who are either physically or mentally ill. People with mental health problems are in pain, are often unable to cope with the daily stress of life, have low self-esteem and feel isolated or alienated. Expressions of their suffering include sitting staring into space on association, neglect of personal hygiene and attempts to harm themselves.

Mental health in prison

There is no shortage of official data on the nature and extent of mental ill health in prison:

- 80 per cent of prisoners have mental health problems;
- 72 per cent of male and 70 per cent of female sentenced prisoners suffer from two or more mental health disorders;
- 40 per cent of male and 63 per cent of female sentenced prisoners have a neurotic disorder;
- 7 per cent of males and 14 per cent of female sentenced prisoners have a psychotic disorder;
- 20 per cent of male and 15 per cent of female sentenced prisoners have previously been admitted to a mental hospital;
- 95 per cent of young prisoners aged 15–21 years suffer from a mental disorder and 80 per cent suffer from at least two such disorders.

(Social Exclusion Unit, 2002)

In April 2006, the Department of Health took full responsibility for the commissioning of prison health care in all (public) prisons. Prison health care is now run by Primary Care Trusts (PCTs) and private prisons must make contracts with the PCT. The aim is to provide equivalence with NHS services in the wider community. But Rickford and Edgar (2005), and others, have argued that there are a number of problems with achieving the goal of equivalence, as follow.

- There are a higher number of mentally ill prisoners when compared to numbers in the community.
- Mentally ill prisoners are confined in the prison hospital or in segregation units.
- Historically, lower quality healthcare services were provided in prisons.

- The prison environment exacerbates the vulnerabilities caused by mental illness.
- Staff may treat mentally ill prisoners as lesser humans, neglecting their needs.
- Less eligibility continues to influence penal policy and wider culture.

Mentally ill people are more likely to be a danger to themselves rather than a danger to others. They are, however, often considered to be dangerous and suffering from dangerous and severe personality disorder (DSPD). This is a diagnosis of exclusion and many clinicians believe that DSPD cannot be treated. At the moment, there are around 2,400 prisoners who are considered to suffer from DSPD. Prison Service Order (PSO) 1700 suggests that anyone on segregation for more than three months should be considered to have a personality disorder (HM Prison Service, 2004). The problems with this direction are that:

- many prisoners with mental illness are placed into segregation unit for long periods, sometimes for their own protection;
- there is no agreed way of assessing DSPD;
- it is a convenient diagnosis that puts individual blame on the prisoner. Some of the most notorious prisoners for control problems have successfully addressed their behaviours—see, for example, Boyle (1977).

> **Common pitfall**   *When looking at prisoner mental health, you will encounter legal, medical and forensic psychology. Ensure you have a dictionary to help you to understand the technical language used.*

Self-inflicted deaths (SIDs)

Imprisonment is plagued by the deaths of prisoners. The following are three tragic examples.

- ***Joseph Scholes*** Joseph died, aged 16, on 24 March 2002 at Stoke Heath YOI. Joseph was being treated for depression and had a history of self-harm. Shortly after his arrival at Stoke Heath, he was moved from its special unit for vulnerable inmates into a cell with bars on its window. He hanged himself from the bars after nine days in custody. Two weeks before sentencing, he had slashed his face thirty times. Despite a recommendation that custody should not be used in Joseph's case, no places were available elsewhere.
- ***Sarah Campbell*** Aged 18, Sarah died of an overdose at HMP and YOI Styal on 18 January 2003. She had been sent to Styal on the previous day. Contrary

to recommendations, Sarah was placed alone in the segregation unit. Denied access to the television, the radio or someone to talk to, her only means of communicating was through a crack in the door. On the morning of her death, Sarah swallowed a large number of anti-depressants and then told staff what she had done. She was left unattended and locked in her cell. Alone, Sarah vomited blood. There was an avoidable delay of around forty minutes between the reporting of the overdose and the arrival of the ambulance. At the inquest in January 2005, the jury returned a damning narrative verdict stating that there had been a '*failure in the duty of care*' (INQUEST, 2007a).

- **Adam Rickwood** Adam was found dead on 9 August 2004 at a secure training centre in Hassockfield in County Durham. He was 14 years old. It was Adam's first time in custody and he had told his mother that he intended to kill himself a few days previously. Adam is the youngest ever person to die in custody.

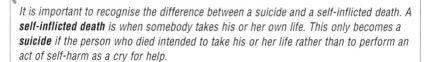

It is important to recognise the difference between a suicide and a self-inflicted death. A **self-inflicted death** *is when somebody takes his or her own life. This only becomes a* **suicide** *if the person who died intended to take his or her life rather than to perform an act of self-harm as a cry for help.*

The number of self-inflicted deaths (SIDs) in prison has risen dramatically during the last 25 years. In 1983, there were 27 self-inflicted deaths in prison in England and Wales. We have, however, seen a steep rise in numbers in recent years, with 91 in 1999, 94 in 2002 and a record number of 95 in 2004 (see Figure 2.3). There were 67 SIDs in 2006. Disturbingly, the rate of deaths has increased once again and, before the end of September 2007, this number had already been exceeded (INQUEST, 2007b).

Who is to blame? Explanations of self-inflicted death

Four main explanations of self-inflicted deaths have been proposed.

1. *High-risk inadequates*, manipulators and attention seekers. The person who has died is personally culpable for their own death. Victims are defined as high-risk inadequates and 'negative reputations' are established (Scraton and Chadwick, 1987). Reflecting an institutionalisation of the doctrine of less eligibility, prisoners are considered to be lesser beings who do not have the same human rights as those of law-abiding people. Rather than focusing on the Prison Service and the responsibilities of the state to care for those in custody, the person who has died is identified

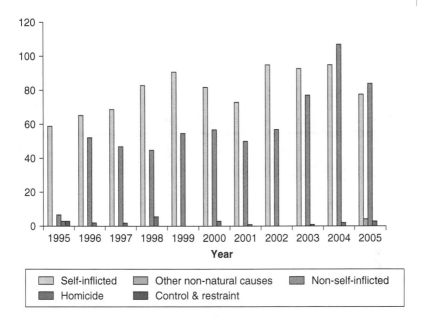

Figure 2.3   Deaths in prison 1995–2005
Source: INQUEST (2006)

as the problem. These 'weak' people would have committed suicide whether they were in prison or not.

2. *Poor prison conditions* An alternative explanation has looked to locate the cause of such deaths within specific institutional problems, such as overcrowding, poor physical conditions, low feelings of safety, or levels of staffing. From this perspective, the prison environment can be healthy and safe, but becomes dangerous when it falls below certain standards.

3. *People vulnerable to prison environment* Prisons are filled with large numbers of people with poor coping skills who are vulnerable to the unpredictability of prison life. SIDs arise from a combination of 'risky prisoners', who may or may not be psychiatrically ill, and their inability to cope with confinement.

4. *Inherent harms and pains of imprisonment* All prisoners are vulnerable, because the isolation, hopelessness and brutality are endemic to prison life. This highly toxic and dehumanising environment cannot be made completely safe or healthy. Its very existence is the negation of human-ity, undermining constructions of the self and the meaning of life.

Illicit substance misuse and infectious diseases

A 'drug' is a chemical substance that can alter your behaviour, emotions or your psychological or physical disposition. Such substances include: LSD (lysergic acid diethylamide), cocaine, alcohol, heroin, tobacco, cannabis, barbiturates, MDMA (3,4-methylenedioxy-N-methylamphetamine) or ecstasy (XTC), methadone, solvents, and caffeine.

What do prisoners and staff think about cannabis?

If the boys want to blow [smoke cannabis] you should let them because it keeps them quiet and they keep their head down.

(Prisoner, cited in Keene, 1997, p. 31)

I think that cannabis is generally accepted and tolerated. It makes inmates quiet, they have a smoke, go to bed and are quite happy and no problem to anyone.

(Prison officer, cited in Keene, 1997, p. 34)

Cannabis calms them down beautifully.

(Prison governor, cited in Seddon, 1996, p. 331)

I think that if I had never had drugs in prison I could never have served my sentence.

(Prisoner, cited in Keene, 1997, p. 31)

Prisoners who use illicit substances are labelled as doubly 'deviant', in that they are viewed both as criminals and as drug (mis)users. Illicit substances enter prisons by a variety of sources. Some of the most common routes include their being smuggled in through visits, by prison officers, administrators or teachers, or through the delivery of supplies and 'drops' over the fence.

Illicit substance use in prison

Number of prisoners who use drugs in prison

- *Cannabis 57%*
- *Heroin 24%*
- *LSD/XTC 16%*

(Continued)

- *Cocaine 15%*
- *Crack 12%*
- *Amphetamines 11%*

(Advisory Council on Misuse of Drugs, 1996)

Profile of illicit substance (mis)user in prison

- Young (average age 23)
- Low socio-economic social background
- Male
- Polydrug use (i.e. uses many different drugs)
- Dependent
- Failed treatments
- In poor physical health
- Contracted infectious disease

The most recent drug policy was set out in HM Prison Service's *Tackling Drugs in Prison: The Prison Service Drug Strategy* (1998b). This is a ten-year strategy and its main priorities are to:

- reduce recidivism among drug-misusing offenders;
- increase referrals for treatment;
- increase treatment programme completion;
- deter and detect drug availability in prisons.

The Counselling, Assessment, Referral, Advice and Throughcare Service (CARATS)

In 1999, the prison service introduced the Counselling, Assessment, Referral, Advice and Throughcare Service (CARATS). CARATS is focused on delivering treatments to drug-using prisoners. It has seven interrelated stages, as follows.

1. Make initial contact on reception.
2. Make referrals to enable clinical assessments and detoxification.
3. Undertake a full assessment, based on prisoner needs.
4. Prepare care plans, with regular care reviews.
5. Counselling and group work to address substance misuse.
6. Planning to help management of drug problem on release.
7. Post-release work to establish links with community-based agencies.

An interlinked problem with illicit substance misuse is the spread of infectious and contagious diseases. One of the most significant is the spread of HIV and AIDS in prison. The rates of HIV are higher in prisons than among the wider population and the situation is getting worse. In 1997, new diagnoses in the general population were at 2,750, but by 2005, this had increased to over 7,000. There are a number of policy options to help to contain the spread of HIV and other infectious diseases, and sexually transmitted diseases (STDs).

- **Condoms** Prisoners must send a 'Dear Doctor' letter to prison medical officers, who can prescribe condoms and lubricants if they judge there to be a genuine risk of HIV transmission. But the process is slow, there is no confidentiality and condoms are not available in around a quarter of prisons.
- **Disinfecting tablets** Prison Service Instruction (PSI) 53/2003 created provisions for tablets that would disinfect shared needles and syringes to be made available to prisoners (HM Prison Service, 2003c). This was officially introduced in April 2004.
- **Needle exchange programmes** The Prison Service has no plans to introduce needle exchange programmes. This is largely because of security concerns that needles would be used as weapons against other prisoners or prison officers. Evidence available from prisons in which needle exchange programmes have been introduced, however, is that they makes prisons safer places because they replace needles that are already in the prison and which may be infected with a disease.
- **Tattooing** There are no plans to provide safe facilities for tattooing.

A report by the Prison Reform Trust/National AIDS Trust (2005) found that HIV-positive prisoners had received inadequate health care, inferior treatment, poor facilities, low levels of medical expertise and badly trained staff who breached confidentiality of their patients.

Keep up to date with HM Prison Service and NOMS policies on substance misuse and contagious diseases.

Towards harm reduction

A key theme in responding to the inherent harms of imprisonment is the principle of harm reduction. This involves the following.

1. Acknowledgement that harmful behaviour is taking place.
2. The need to understand why behaviour occurs.

(Continued)

3. Raising awareness of harms inherent in certain behaviour, but involving the suspension of moral judgement or of a focus on abstention.
4. Reducing the negative consequences arising from the harm.
5. Aiming to increase the safety of all concerned, potentially including safer ways of doing certain harm.
6. Empowering the person who has undertaken the harm.
7. Reducing risks of the harmer repeating behaviour.
8. Focusing on quality of life as measurement of success.

(Derived from PRT/NAT, 2005)

"Is prison culture imported or is it created through the deprivations of prison life?"

This question is asking you to consider the classic works of Clemmer (1948) and Sykes (1958). Firstly, you will need to identify the arguments supporting the close association of prison culture with the culture and background of those who are imprisoned. You should then consider the specific problems that are created by and within the penal environment. You might wish to highlight how prison culture is also shaped by wider dominant norms and values in society as a whole.

Taking it **FURTHER**

There are a number of other important sociological studies of prison life. Check your university library to see which of the following are available. (These studies are some of the most accessible and interesting books on prisons.)

- Bowker, L (1977) *Prisoner Subcultures*, Lexington, MA: DC Heath and Co
- Carrabine, E (2004) *Power, Discourse and Resistance*, Aldershot: Ashgate Publishing
- Cressey, R (1959) *The Prison*, New York: Anchor Press
- Dilulio, JJ (1990) *Governing Prisons*, London :Free Press
- Emery, FE (1970) *Freedom and Justice Within Walls*, London: Tavistock

(Continued)

- Fitzgerald, M and Sim, J (1982) British Prisons, 2nd edn, Oxford: Blackwell
- Hobhouse, S and Brockway, AF (1922) *English Prisons Today*, London: Longmans, Green and Co
- Irwin, J (1970) *The Felon*, Englewood Cliffs, NJ: Prentice Hall
- Jacobs, JB (1978) *Stateville*, Chicago, IL: University of Chicago
- Jewkes, Y (2002) *Captive Audience*, Cullompton: Willan Publishing
- Jones, H and Cornes, P (1973) *Open Prisons*, London: Routledge Kegan Paul
- King, R and Elliott, K (1977) *Albany*, London: Routledge Kegan Paul
- Lombardo, LX (1981) *Guards Imprisoned*, New York: Elsevier
- Mathiesen, T (1965) *Defences of the Weak*, London: Tavistock
- Morris, TP and Morris, P (1963) *Pentonville*, London: Routledge Kegan Paul
- Scraton, P et al. (1991) *Prisons Under Protest*, Milton Keynes: Open University Press
- Sparks, R et al. (1996) *Prisons and the Problem of Order*, Oxford: Clarendon Press
- Thomas, JE (1972) *The Prison Office*, London: Routledge Kegan Paul
- Toch, H (1975) *Men in Crisis*, Chicago, IL: Aldine
- Toch, H (1977) *Living in Prison*, New York: Free Press

Textbook guide

CAVADINO, M AND DIGNAN, J (2007) The Penal System, 4th edn, London: Sage

COYLE, A (2005) Understanding Prisons, Milton Keynes: Open University Press

FLYNN, N. (1998) Introduction to Prisons and Imprisonment, Winchester: Waterside Press

JEWKES, Y (ED) (2007a) Handbook of Prisons, Cullompton: Willan Publishing

JEWKES, Y AND JOHNSON, H (EDS) (2006) Prison Readings: A Critical Introduction to Prisons and Imprisonment, Cullompton: Willan Publishing

MATTHEWS, R (1999) Doing Time, London: Palgrave

SCOTT, DG AND CODD, H (2008) Controversial Issues In Prison, Milton Keynes: Open University Press

2.9	
penal accountability	

Core areas: **the exercise of penal power**

the stewardship model: financial and managerial accountability

inspection at home: HMIP, IMB and the PPO

legal accountability: prison rules, prison law and the HRA

international and regional protection: CPT, the ECHR and the UN

 Running themes

- Human rights
- Legitimacy
- Managerialism
- Power to punish
- Social justice

Key penologists

Baron David John Ramsbotham (born 1934) Nicknamed 'Rambo', Baron Ramsbotham grew up in County Durham and is the son of the former Bishop of Wakefield. He was a general in the British Army and served in Northern Ireland, before being appointed as HM Chief Inspector of Prisons for England and Wales (HMCIP) from 1995–2001. A controversial figure, he has had a strained relationship with government. He famously led a Lords' revolt against the abolition of HMIP in 2006 and is author of the highly critical book, *Prisongate* (2003). He is currently president of UNLOCK (the National Association of Reformed Offenders), and vice chair of both the All Party Penal Affairs Group and the All Party Parliamentary Group for Learning and Skills in the Criminal Justice System.

Judge Sir Steven Tumin (1930–2003) The son of an assize court clerk, Judge Tumin grew up in wartime Oxford, where he had a lonely childhood due to the death of his mother when he was aged only 10 years. He became a county court circuit judge in 1978. As HM Chief Inspector of Prisons (HMCIP) from 1987–1995, he proved to be a staunch critic of the government and a passionate advocate of humanitarian penal reforms. He was co-author, with Lord Woolf, of Part II of the famous investigation into the disturbances at Strangeways prison (published 1991) and author of a number of tracts on penal reform. In retirement, Tumin was chairman of the Koestler Award Trust and also served as president of UNLOCK. He died suddenly in December 2003, aged 73.

Sir Nigel Rodley (born 1941) From 1973–1990, Sir Nigel Rodley was a senior legal adviser for Amnesty International and, from 1993–2001, he was United Nations (UN) Special Rapporteur on Torture. Educated at Leeds University, Nigel Rodley was also awarded a PhD from the University of Essex. His major publications include *The Treatment of Prisoners under International Law* (first published in 1987). He is currently a member of the UN Human Rights Committee and Professor and Chair of the Human Rights Centre, University of Essex.

The exercise of penal power

When thinking about punishment—that is, the deliberate infliction of pain—questions of legitimacy are central to any debate. To be legally and democratically accountable is a key part of any legitimate response to dealing with social harms, problems and wrongdoing.

> *It may come as a surprise to you to discover that there is very little literature on prison accountability and that much of what currently exists was written in the 1980s or 1990s.*

Accountability, for the pro-prison lobby, has been largely reduced to concerns around cost-effectiveness and ensuring that the delivery of punishment represents value for money. Liberal penologists have accepted the right of the state to punish, but are concerned that penal power is used correctly. Although anti-prison critics have questioned the very basis of the power to punish, arguing that no one has the right to harm another person, like the liberal penologists, they are interested in how state power is held to account and in the effectiveness of formal mechanisms that are in place to 'guard the guards'.

The stewardship model: financial and managerial accountability

The first approach to accountability is to ensure that the sums add up. This *financial* accountability involves scrutiny of Prison Service accounts and is detailed in the Prison Service's annual report. The 'stewardship model' has, however, gained increasing importance with the rise of managerialism. Tied to the principles of economy, efficiency and effectiveness, it involves an increasing focus on reducing costs and increasing performance through standards, and through key performance indicators (KPIs) and targets. The problem is that, under this managerial model, you can find out the cost of everything—but end up understanding the value of nothing.

> The Prison Service is relatively transparent about its finances. This can lead to a discussion of the cost-effectiveness and fiscal logic of penal expansionism.

Inspection at home: HMIP, IMB and the PPO

There are three domestic forms of penal accountability in England and Wales:

- Her Majesty's Inspectorate of Prisons (HMIP);
- the Independent Monitoring Board (IMB);
- the Prison and Probation Ombudsman (PPO).

While at first appearing to provide a strong form of accountability, questions have been raised about the power of these institutions to hold the government to account, their independence and in whose interests they serve. Critics point to the difference between paying 'lip service' and legitimating imprisonment, and genuine forms of penal accountability.

- ***Her Majesty's Inspectorate of Prisons for England and Wales (HMIP)*** HMIP reports on the conditions of those held in prison, young offender institutions and immigration centres. Appointed by the Home Secretary, the current HM Chief Inspector of Prisons (HMCIP) is Anne Owers. Section 5A of the Prison Act 1952 sets out the responsibilities for her role (see s. 57 of the Criminal Justice Act 1982). The HMIP was established by the May Committee in 1979 and has had some high-profile chief inspectors, including Judge Stephen Tumin and Baron David Ramsbotham. The HMIP carries out full inspections, full follow-up inspections and short follow-up inspections. Alongside these individual inspections, the HMIP produces an annual report and regular thematic studies, on issues such as on suicide or racism.

Healthy prisons

Since 1999, the HMIP has used 'healthy prison' criteria to assess the moral legitimacy of a penal regime. The four key tests are as follows.

- *Safety* Prisoners, even the most vulnerable, are held safely.
- *Respect* Prisoners are treated with respect for their human dignity.
- *Purposeful activity* Prisoners are able, and expected, to engage in activity that is likely to benefit them.
- *Resettlement* Prisoners are prepared for release into the community and helped to reduce the likelihood of their reoffending.

(HMCIP, 1999)

The HMIP has only limited powers and can neither hold the Prison Service to legal account nor enforce changes, but it does provide an important shaming function, consistently producing damning reports of dreadful prison conditions. In 2006, the government attempted to abolish the HMIP, but this proposal was rejected by the House of Lords.

Common pitfall *There are a large number of inspection reports published each year and it is easy to lose motivation when examining so many documents. To avoid overload, read the annual report and then individual reports that have been highlighted in the media. Also look at the thematic reports that are published regularly by the HMIP, such as those on suicide, race relations or mental health.*

- **Independent Monitoring Board (IMB)** The IMB comprises unpaid volunteers who are appointed by Home Office Ministers to monitor the day-to-day life of penal institutions in their local area. Every prison has an IMB.

Known as 'Boards of Visitors' (BoV) until 2004, the Independent Monitoring Board (IMB) has a long history in prisons in England and Wales.

Until the early 1990s, the IMB had a disciplinary function, as well as a monitoring role. Its disciplinary role had, however, been legally challenged since the 1970s and was ended by the Woolf Report (1991). To address claims that the BoV were *'in the pocket of the government'*, the organisation changed its name to the 'Independent Monitoring Board'. Current members of the IMB are charged with ensuring that proper standards of care and decency are maintained in prison, and can also deal with confidential requests from prisoners. IMB volunteers are supposed to have unrestricted access to all areas and can talk to any prisoner or detainee they wish. To continue in their role, IMB volunteers must regularly attend their given prison and each IMB must produce an annual report. The IMB can play an important role as a whistleblower, highlighting brutality in prisons through its annual report, but it has no formal powers to hold an institution to account; it has only an advisory function. IMBs are *not* independent, however, and impartiality is also hampered through the close relationships that volunteers often develop with prison staff. Unsurprisingly, prisoners do not always trust IMB volunteers, seeing them as working in the interests of the prison rather than those of the prisoners. Although there are exceptions, most members of the IMB are middle-aged and middle class, and neither represent the wider community nor have much in common with the social backgrounds of prisoners.

• **Prison and Probation Ombudsman (PPO)** The PPO investigates complaints from prisoners and, since 2001, those subject to probation supervision. The Ombudsman does not have any statutory powers, and is appointed to exercise the Home Secretary's powers on prisons and prisoners. This means that the Home Secretary can have great influence on how the Ombudsman undertakes its role and this undermines its claims to independence. The role was introduced in 1994, but, after a row between Sir Peter Woodhead, then Ombudsman, and Michael Howard, then Home Secretary, in 1996, a number of powers were taken away. New terms of reference were introduced in 2001, but these still impose considerable restraints.

The Ombudsman will examine complaints to consider whether they are eligible. To assist in this process, where there is some doubt or dispute as to the eligibility of a complaint, the Ombudsman will inform the Prison Service or the National Probation Service Area Board of the complaint and, where necessary, the Prison Service or area board will then provide the Ombudsman with such documents or other information as the Ombudsman considers are relevant to considering eligibility.

(Home Office, cited in Livingstone et al., 2003, p. 50)

The current Ombudsman is Stephen Shaw, and he is responsible for investigating deaths of prisoners, immigration detainees and residents of probation hostels. The Ombudsman produces annual reports and has carried out high-profile investigations into controversial incidents, such as the death of Harold Shipman and the disturbances at Yarlswood immigration centre. The Ombudsman's powers are limited to making recommendations to the chief executive of NOMS and it cannot comment on any decisions made by Ministers.

Legal accountability: prison rules, prison law and the HRA

> ### The Prison Act 1952
>
> The authority of penal administrators is derived largely, but not exclusively, from the Prison Act 1952, a statutory framework that confers massive discretionary powers upon penal officials. It is essentially enabling legislation, outlining who is legally empowered to perform duties relating to the operation and management of prisons.

Section 47 of the Prison Act 1952 provides for the Home Secretary to make rules for the regulation and management of prisons; the resulting Prison Rules 1999 outline the procedures, policy objectives and obligations of the prison authorities. Lord Denning, in *Becker v Home Office* (1972), famously claimed that '*the prison rules are regulatory directions only. Even if they are not observed, they do not give rise to a cause of action*' (cited in Scott, 2006, p. 122). This implied that prison rules did not give rights to prisoners. Recently, however, there have been movements to recognise that prison rules and also other non-statutory instruments, such as Prison Service Orders (PSOs) and Prison Service Instructions (PSIs), do, in fact, infer certain obligations onto the state and legal rights for prisoners.

> ### A legal right
>
> An assertion is a legal right when the claim is protected and sanctioned through the law. Consequently, prisoners' legal rights can be understood as those legally enforceable claims that require the accomplishment or restraint of certain actions on the part of the Prison Service.

While coming to such a definition is relatively straightforward, determining the content and interpretation of such rights for prisoners has proved to be much more controversial. Indeed, even the very acknowledgement that prisoners possess some legal rights has been highly contested. For example, up until the 1970s, prisoners were considered to possess only privileges and, once the gate closed behind them, were viewed as being beyond normal legal remedies.

The policies of penal administrators were uncritically supported or condoned by a highly conservative, non-interventionist legal discourse, with a self-imposed deference to the executive. While some cases were successful, prisons were left to themselves, becoming lawless and discretionary institutions with which the use of arbitrary powers by staff could go largely unchecked. This attitude gradually began to change in the 1970s and 1980s, with a gradual shift towards the recognition that prisoners do have some legal rights. The current basis of prisoners' residual legal rights can be found in Lord Wilberforce's definitive statement in *Raymond v Honey* (1982), within which he stated that a prisoner *'retains all civil rights which are not taken away expressly or by necessary implication'* (cited in Scott, 2006, p. 123).

Human Rights Act 1998

- *Article 2* Right to life
- *Article 3* Prohibition of torture
- *Article 4* Prohibition of forced labour and slavery
- *Article 5* Right to liberty and security
- *Article 6* Right to a fair trial
- *Article 7* No punishment without law
- *Article 8* Right to respect for private and family life
- *Article 9* Freedom of thought, conscience and religion
- *Article 10* Freedom of expression
- *Article 11* Freedom of assembly and association
- *Article 12* Right to marry
- *Article 14* Prohibition of discrimination
- *Article 16* Restrictions on political activities of aliens
- *Article 17* Prohibition of abuse of rights
- *Article 18* Limitations on use of restrictions on rights

First Protocol

- *Article 1* Protection of property
- *Article 2* Right to education
- *Article 3* Right to free elections

Sixth Protocol

- *Article 1* Abolition of death penalty
- *Article 2* Death penalty in time of war

On the 2 October 2000, the Human Rights Act (HRA) 1998 was implemented. The HRA incorporates the European Convention on Human Rights (ECHR) into English law. Under the HRA, all new primary legislation, and existing procedures and practices of public authorities, must be compatible with the principles of the ECHR. Despite great hopes that the HRA would lead to an expansion of prisoners' legal rights, in the years since it was introduced and despite a handful of victories for prisoners, very little has changed. In the period both before and after the introduction of the HRA, cases have been most successful when they:

- fall within an area of traditional judicial intervention, such as those of legal advice and access, or release and discipline;
- raise concerns regarding natural justice, due process or procedural issues;
- aim to provide greater transparency in the decision-making process of penal administrators.

Where prisoners' claims have failed—the most common finding—the domestic courts in both private and public law have often justified such a decision through submitting to the arguments that such a restriction is required because of necessary implications, or by showing support for the convenience of those administering imprisonment. In judgments relating to interference with Convention rights, prison authorities have maintained the courts' sympathy in terms of their requirements for discretionary decision making, or on the basis that the restriction is necessary on grounds of prison security, order, the needs of victims of crime, the prevention of crime and even administrative convenience.

Absolute rights of a prisoner

When we ask the question 'what absolute rights are invested in prisoners?', the answer remains fairly brief. Prisoners in England and Wales have the absolute right to commence legal proceedings at an impartial and independent tribunal, and must be allowed uninhibited access to legal advice, whether through legal visits or correspondence.

Prisoner rights jurisprudence can be developed to make a substantial impact on prisoners' lived realities, but the domestic courts must first recognise that no human being should have to live in the appalling circumstances in which many prisoners find themselves today.

> **Common pitfall** *To understand the legal rights of prisoners fully requires some under-standing of the law. If you are a social science or humanities student, ensure that you get guidance from the law librarian before you start to look at recent case law.*

International and regional protection: CPT, the ECHR and the UN

Outside of the domestic forms of accountability, there are regional and international bodies to which prisoners can appeal to uphold legal rights, and to hold the state and its penal authorities to account. At the regional level (Europe), there are the European Court of Human Rights (ECtHR) and the Committee for the Prevention of Torture (CPT); at the international level, there are various bodies that have been established by the United Nations (UN).

- **The European Court of Human Rights (ECtHR)** The ECtHR was established in Strasbourg in 1951 by the European Convention on Human Rights (ECHR). Prisoner petitions to the ECtHR have been successful since the 1970s. It was expected that, with the introduction of the HRA, the ECtHR would be less sig-nificant in defining and upholding prisoners rights, but, because the UK courts have conservatively interpreted the HRA, the ECtHR has continued to be the main progressive legal avenue for prisoners. Recent successes have included cases on mandatory sentences (*Stafford* (2002)), inquiries into deaths in cus-tody (*Edwards* (2002)), governor adjudications (*Ezeh and Connors* (2002)) and the right to vote (*Hirst* (2004)). The main drawback of the ECtHR, and of the ECHR generally, is that it has a very restrictive understanding of human rights and has largely supported prisoners when procedural, rather than substan-tive, rights have been breached.
- **The Committee for the Prevention of Torture (CPT)** The CPT was created by Article 1 of the European Convention for the Prevention of Torture and Inhuman or Degrading Treatment or Punishment (1987). The Committee, com-prising penal experts from across Europe, visits penal establishments among the 46 countries of the Council of Europe that have ratified the Treaty. The focus of the CPT includes all places of detention (e.g. prisons and juvenile detention centres, police stations, holding centres for immigration detainees and psychiatric hospitals) and aims to highlight cases in which it feels that confinement is inhuman, degrading or amounting to torture. All visits are undertaken after prior notification, but this notification may be made directly before the visit is about to take place. CPT delegates should have unlimited access to designated places of detention and the right to move inside without

restriction. The primary goal of the CPT is the prevention of torture and it reports directly to the government of the member State under investigation. The CPT does not provide the public shaming of abusing States, but is instead guided by the principles of co-operation and confidentiality. Only if a country fails to co-operate will the CPT make a public statement. The CPT has visited the United Kingdom on three occasions—most recently, investigating the conditions of terrorist suspects at HMP Belmarsh. The CPT has been said to be a 'toothless tiger', however, and its reports have done little to add to the jurisprudence on torture, inhuman and degrading treatment or to improve the lived realities of prisoners in the United Kingdom.

Common pitfall   *The CPT reports are important, but you will find that they follow a very similar pattern. Report writers are heavily reliant upon 'cut and paste', so be selective of the reports you read.*

- ***United Nations (UN)*** The UN is an international body that has produced a number of major Declarations, Charters, standards and principles outlining international law on prison conditions. The 1948 United Nations Declaration and the 1966 Convention on Civil and Political Rights feature Articles that condemn torture and cruel, inhuman or degrading treatment; the 1966 Convention also states that *'all persons deprived of liberty shall be treated with humanity and with respect for the inherent dignity of the person'*. In 1955, the UN introduced the Standard Minimum Rules for the Treatment of Prisoners and, in 1988, it published the Body of Principles for the Protection of All Persons Under Any Form of Detention or Imprisonment. In addition, the UN has a Special Rapporteur and Committee for the Prevention of Torture (see above).

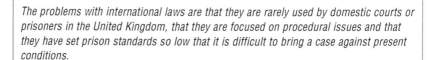

The problems with international laws are that they are rarely used by domestic courts or prisoners in the United Kingdom, that they are focused on procedural issues and that they have set prison standards so low that it is difficult to bring a case against present conditions.

❝ Does Her Majesty's Chief Inspector of Prisons have enough power to hold the Prison Service to account? ❞

You must first outline the main role and duties of the HMCIP, and then identify the powers that it has to hold the Prison Service to account. Provide a critical scrutiny and identify how the current powers are relatively limited. Identify the main themes of some recent reports, and also look at the comments of the current and former HMCIPs. To conclude, provide some indication of what would be necessary to a HMIP that could hold the Prison Service to account.

Taking it **FURTHER**

Read an official report of your local prison by either the HMCIP or the IMB. What does the report say about the prison? Is it critical? Does it indicate whether previous recommendations have been acted upon? Does the report get to the heart of the running of the prison and the problems that are encountered there?

Textbook guide

CREIGHTON, S, KING, V AND ARNOTT, H **(2005)** *Prisoners and the Law*, 3rd edn, Haywards Heath: Tottel Publishing

FITZGERALD, M AND SIM, J **(1982)** *British Prisons*, 2nd edn, Oxford: Blackwell

HARDING, R **(1997)** *Private Prisons and Public Accountability*, Milton Keynes: Open University Press

LIVINGSTONE, S, OWEN, T AND MACDONALD, A **(2003)** *Prison Law*, 3rd edn, Oxford: Oxford University Press

MAGUIRE, M, VAGG, J AND MORGAN, R (EDS) **(1985)** *Accountability and Prisons: Opening Up a Closed World*, London: Tavistock

RODLEY, N **(1999)** *The Treatment of Prisoners Under International Law*, 2nd edn, Oxford: Clarendon Press

VAGG, J **(1994)** *Prison Systems: A Comparative Study of Accountability in England, France, Germany and The Netherlands*, Oxford: Clarendon Press

2.10

probation and community penalties

Core areas: **advise, assist, and befriend: the history of probation**
corrections: the current role of the National Probation Service
offender management
community penalties
towards decarceration?

Running themes

- Alternatives to prison
- Legitimacy
- Managerialism
- Penal reform
- Power to punish
- Rehabilitation
- Risk

Key penologists

Professor Sir Anthony Bottoms Tony Bottoms was Wolfson Professor of Criminology at the University of Cambridge from 1984 to 2006. He is a leading figure in penology, and has written extensively on prisons and alternatives to custody. His most recent books include (with Richard Sparks and Will Hay) *Prisons and the Problem of Order* (1992) and *Alternatives to Prison* (2004), the latter in collaboration with Sue Rex and Gwen Robinson. He was elected Fellow of the British Academy in 1997.

Professor Stan Cohen Stan Cohen was Martin White Professor of Sociology at the London School of Economics from 1996 to 2006 before Parkinson's disease enforced his early retirement. Cohen grew up in South Africa and was an undergraduate at the University of Witwatersrand. He worked as a social worker in

London before undertaking a PhD at the London School of Economics. Cohen taught at the University of Durham and the University of Essex, before he moved with his family to Israel in 1980. In Israel, he was a human rights activist and director of the Institute of Criminology at the Hebrew University. Perhaps the most influential writer on crime and punishment of his generation, Stan Cohen has written on moral panics, prisons, social control, human rights and the techniques we deploy to deny the suffering of others. He was elected as a member of the British Academy in 1987 and received the Sellin-Glueck Prize from the American Society of Criminology in 1985. His most recent book, *States of Denial* (2001), was voted best book of that year by the British Academy in 2002.

Professor Andrew Scull Distinguished Professor of Sociology as Social Science at the University of California since 1994, Andrew Scull studied as an undergraduate at Oxford University from 1966–1969 and was awarded a PhD from Princeton in 1974. He is one of the leading writers on history, psychiatry, medicine and social control. His books include *Decarceration* (1977), *Museums of Madness* (1979) and, with John Andrews, *Undertaker of the Mind* (2001).

Advise, assist and befriend: the history of probation

The Probation Service performs a key role within the penal system. In recent times, it has become increasingly aligned with the Prison Service and both are now tied through the National Offender Management Service. Probation does, however, have a very different history to that of the prison.

Probation arose in the nineteenth century, as a result of voluntary, ad hoc and informal attempts to provide support, friendship, and spiritual and practical guidance for offenders. One of the most significant forms of philanthropy came from the police court missionaries who were employed by the Church of England Temperance Society in the 1870s to help to rehabilitate alcoholics. The idea of probation for offenders was first introduced in 1877, but the most significant piece of legislation came with the Probation of Offenders Act 1907. This empowered every court to appoint at least one probation officer whose role was to '*advise, assist and befriend*' offenders. The probation officer had a direct supervisory role, and was there to assist the offender in leading an industrious, peaceful, well-behaved and lawful life. The Criminal Justice Act 1948 led to a greater professionalisation of the Probation Service, laying down guidelines for training and improved links with the courts, introducing new probation hostels and allowing for their administration through new probation committees. There were 54 probation committees, comprising magistrates, judges, civil servants and representatives of the local community.

It is important that you examine closely the changes between the historic role of probation and its current deployment in the criminal justice system. This can also help you to track wider changes in crime control.

Corrections: the current role of the National Probation Service

The Probation Service has undergone considerable changes in recent times. In April 2001, the National Probation Service of England and Wales (NPS) was launched. The NPS has 42 operational areas that are equivalent to the boundaries of the Police and Crown Prosecution Services. There has also been a considerable change in the perceived role and functions of the Probation Service. Rather than befriending offenders, today, probation officers are expected to help to assess and manage risk.

The role of the NPS is to:

- provide pre-sentence reports to the courts;
- supervise offenders in the community;
- manage offender programmes and reduce the risk of reoffending;
- safeguard the welfare of children;
- facilitate crime prevention initiatives;
- undertake work in prison.

The work of the NPS is extensive.

- There are over a hundred approved probation hostels for offenders on bail, community sentences and post-custody licence.
- Each year, the Probation Service supervises 175,000 offenders.
- The caseload on any given day is in excess of 200,000 (90 per cent of whom are male and 10 per cent are female).
- Seventy per cent of offenders supervised are on community sentences.
- Each year, the Probation Service provides 246,000 pre-sentence reports and 20,000 bail information reports.
- Each year, the Probation Service writes 87,000 risk assessment reports.

Offender management

Probation officers have undertaken work in prisons since 1966, but the two 'correctional' services have become more closely intertwined in recent times. The momentum for recent changes has been driven by the sentencing implications of the Halliday Report (2001), the emphasis on cognitive behaviouralism in the 'What Works' agenda, and the belief that problems in the criminal justice system can be solved through more effective management and the introduction of competition. The end result of this is that NOMS now manages both the Prison and Probation Services, and that, through the principle of 'contestability', the delivery of community penalties are opened up to market testing. Following the Halliday Review, the Criminal Justice Act 2003 tied punishments served in prison and the community together, indicating that the most significant differences between prison and probation officers is now in where they perform their correctional duties, rather than in their task or work ethos.

Look at the NPS website, and read the NPS and NOMS annual report. You will also find the National Association of Probation Officers (NAPO) useful.

Community penalties

Non-custodial sanctions can be divided between those that require supervision and those that do not.

*Examples of current penalties with **no supervision** include:*

- *warnings;*
- *formal cautions;*
- *conditional cautions;*
- *conditional discharge;*
- *fines;*
- *fixed penalty notices;*
- *binding over.*

There are also community penalties that require some form of state supervision or control. These community penalties gained increasing political importance in the 1970s and 1980s, and were tied with the ideas of 'bifurcation'—i.e. the attempt to distinguish between serious and dangerous offenders, who should be imprisoned, and lesser offenders, who should be dealt with through discharges, financial penalties and community sentences (Bottoms, 1977).

The community sentence

The deployment of community penalties has been significantly changed following the Criminal Justice Act 2003. A new generic community sentence was introduced in April 2005. There are three punishment bands: low; medium; and high. The new community sentence can combine a number of requirements in order to punish, rehabilitate, protect society or provide some form of reparation to the victim. The requirements of community sentence can involve:

- unpaid work;
- drug rehabilitation;
- alcohol treatment;
- attendance centre;
- curfews.

Common pitfall   *There have been a number of significant changes to community penalties in recent years. Always ensure that you are up to date with criminal justice terminology: look at recent legislation, and also look at an organisation's website and recent publications to ensure that the work you cite in essays is relevant and correct.*

Towards decarceration?

When talking about 'non-custodial penal sanctions', we are referring to what is known as 'decarceration'. The decarceration movement had considerable influence among both academia—popularised by the influential social theorist, Andrew Scull—and among penal practitioners in the 1960s and 1970s. Decarcerationists called for the closing down of asylums, prisons and reformatories, and their replacement by alternatives rooted in the community.

The destructuring impulse

Cognitive

1. Prisons are costly and ineffective: community penalties are cheaper than prison sentences.
2. Community alternatives must obviously be better—or, at the very least, no worse.
3. In times of overcrowding, community sanctions might ease the pressure on the Prison Service.

Theoretical

1. Insights under labelling theory point to the counterproductivity of control systems.
2. Informal social controls—i.e. family, community, school, economic system—work.
3. We should aim for 'reintegration' (the new panacea).

Ideological

1. There are criticisms of bureaucracy and the penetration of formal controls.
2. There are many doubts about expertise and state intervention.
3. We need to focus on 'less harm' rather than 'more good'.

(Cohen, 1985)

Underscored by a humanitarian ideology, the decarceration vision called for an inclusionary, rather than an exclusionary, mode of social control. But Stan Cohen (1985) identified that, even in its heyday, the decarceration movement proved to be nothing more than a smokescreen for more insidious forms of social control. In fact, in the 1970s, the original structures of social control became stronger, extending their reach, intensity and intrusion, and drawing new 'deviants' into the clutches of their centralised and bureaucratic penalties. The little decarceration that did take place revolved around the mentally ill. This decarceration was actually in response to fiscal pressures and the retrenchment of welfare policies, and alternatives to custody became simply add-ons to the current mechanisms of social control.

Cohen points to problems around the following factors.

- **Net widening** Alternatives to prison can bring new people into the system who have committed minor offences.
- **Thinning mesh** It becomes harder to escape from state controls.
- **Blurring of boundaries** It becomes more difficult to determine institutional and non-institutional forms of control.
- **Penetration** New forms of control go deeper into the social body.

Penalties in the community have become a new way of introduction into the penal system, thus expanding the 'net' for those at the bottom end of the system.

During this time, the prison became defined more negatively—as a warehouse for incorrigibles and hard cases—but continued to expand on a new incapacitative set of logic; overall, the system enlarged itself due to the proliferation of 'soft' community alternatives. This principle of bifurcation and increased community interventions leads, for Cohen to yet '*another round in the game of blaming the victim*' (1985, p. 126).

> From the foundation of the control system, a single principle has governed every form of classification, screening selection, diagnosis, prediction, typology and policy. This is the structural principle of binary opposition: how to sort out the good from the bad, the elect from the damned, the sheep from the goats, the amenable from the non-amenable, the treatable from the non-treatable, the good risks from the bad risks, the high prediction scorers from the low prediction scorers; how to know who belongs in the deep end, who in the shallow end, and who is hard and who is soft.

(Cohen, 1985, p. 86)

*You can make important connections between notions of **dangerousness**, the principle of **bifurcation** and recent debates on **risk** and **actuarial justice**.*

Alternatives, then, may not used as alternatives, but may instead be about making social controls better. It is certainly understandable to be sceptical about alternatives to prison. Thomas Mathiesen (1974) argued that we should not offer a blueprint of the alternative, and should only critique and provide an alternative after the prison system has been dismantled. Mathiesen believed in alternatives, but that penal critics must be strategic to avoid state manipulation. The limitations of this position are that, if critics do not offer a plausible alternative to prison, then they are unlikely to convince the public that they are serious. There must be plausible answers and solutions to social problems, and the reconstruction of the possibility of a better way of dealing with conflicts than that which we currently have now.

The above problems should not lead to nihilism, pessimism or the rejection of alternatives. Stan Cohen puts it best when he states:

> I believe that the ideology of doing good remains powerful ... This is the essence of humanistic civilisation: to exert power and to do good at the same time.

(1985, p. 114)

Common pitfall *Criticism of the 'alternative' has sometimes been described as 'left pessimism' or 'nihilism'. This criticism is probably unfair, because many of the critics of alternatives—such as Mathiesen and Cohen—have continued, in their work and activism, to call for humanitarian changes and a more sophisticated understanding of the positives and limitations of alternatives to custody.*

❝What is "decarceration"? Is there evidence that the USA and the United Kingdom adopted this policy in the 1970s?❞

You will first need to define the term 'decarceration'. Then, look at the evidence of a movement away from using state institutions to deal with human problems. You will find the work of Scull (1977) useful here. Consider also those who have raised question marks against the decarceration thesis. The most detailed and sympathetic to the original argument is Cohen (1985). You may wish to conclude by considering alternative explanations of changes in the 1970s.

Taking it *FURTHER*

Beyond the criminal law: antisocial behaviour

Antisocial behaviour is defined by the government as including a variety of '*complex, selfish and unacceptable activities*' (Home Office, 2006) that blight the quality of life of other people in the community. It is claimed that it provides a breeding ground for future criminal activity. For the government, antisocial behaviour entails:

(Continued)

- rowdy and nuisance behaviour;
- yobbish behaviour and intimidating groups taking over public spaces;
- groups of youths behaving aggressively in shopping precincts;
- neighbours who do not clean up after their dogs;
- vandalism, graffiti and fly-posting;
- people dealing and buying drugs on the street;
- people dumping rubbish and abandoning cars;
- begging and antisocial drinking;
- the misuse of fireworks.

The government believes that the causes of antisocial behaviour include poor parenting, low educational achievement, truancy, community breakdown, early involvement in drug and alcohol misuse, vandalism, lack of social commitment and peer pressures that condone illegalities. Interventions aimed at tackling antisocial behaviour include:

- Warning letters and interviews, contracts and agreements;
- Individual support orders;
- Agreements, contracts and fixed penalty notices;
- Youth-specific interventions;
- Antisocial behaviour orders (ASBOs);
- 'crack house' closure orders;
- possession proceedings against a tenant.

Central to the responses to antisocial behaviour is the government's Respect Action Plan, launched by Tony Blair, then Prime Minister, in January 2006. For Blair, the Plan aims to 'eradicate the scourge of antisocial behaviour', based on his belief that the latter is caused by a breakdown of respect in society and where 'the self-reinforcing bonds of traditional community life do not exist in the same way' (Home Office, 2006). The Plan aimed to tackle antisocial behaviour and to reclaim communities for the law-abiding majority.

Provisions of the Respect Action Plan

- Increase fixed penalty notices for antisocial behaviour from £80 to £100.
- Extend the use of conditional cautions, so that offenders might be required to undertake unpaid community service.
- Provide a lower threshold for seizure of suspected proceeds of crime from £5,000 to £1,000.
- Create new powers to 'shut and seal' premises (including homes) that are a constant source of antisocial behaviour.

(Continued)

- Provide a network of intensive support schemes for problem families, with sanctions to cut Housing Benefit.
- Extend parenting schemes and a national parenting academy to train social workers.
- Allow schools to apply for parenting orders for families of pupils who seriously misbehave in school.
- Give police community support officers the powers to take part in truancy sweeps.
- Introduce national youth volunteering schemes and expand mentoring projects.

(Home Office, 2006)

There are, however, a number of criticisms that can be made about responses to antisocial behaviour. We would appear to be witnessing the growing disciplinary powers of state control that is beyond the legal boundaries of the criminal justice system and that thus presents a serious threat to our civil liberties. Specifically, fixed penalty notices raise concerns centring on the denial of due process rights and the manner in which 'justice' is defined exclusively as successful prosecution. Further, the explanations for antisocial behaviour are rooted in individual and social pathologies that ignore wider social structures, and there is no discussion of the antisocial behaviour of the rich and powerful, which may be more dangerous and damaging to society as a whole.

Textbook guide

BOTTOMS, A, REX, S AND ROBINSON, G (EDS) (2004) *Alternatives to Prison*, Cullompton: Willan Publishing

BROWNLEE, I (1998) *Community Punishment: A Critical Introduction*, London: Longman

COHEN, S (1985) *Visions of Social Control*, Cambridge: Polity Press

GARLAND, D AND YOUNG, P (EDS) (1983) *The Power to Punish: Contemporary Penality and Social Analysis*, London: Heinemann Educational Books

GELSTHORPE, L AND MORGAN, R (EDS) (2007) *Handbook of Probation*, Cullompton: Willan Publishing

RAYNOR, P AND VANSTONE, M (2002) *Understanding Community Penalties*, Milton Keynes: Open University Press

WORRALL, A AND HOY, C (2005) *Punishment in the Community*, Cullompton: Willan Publishing

2.11

future directions and alternative visions

Core areas: **penal expansionism and 'prison works'**
penal standstill
penal reductionism
penal abolitionism
thinking critically about penal legitimacy
radical alternatives

Running themes

- Alternatives to prison
- Human rights
- Legitimacy
- Pains of imprisonment
- Power to punish
- Social divisions
- Social justice

Key penologists

Charles Murray (born 1943) Currently associated with the American Enterprise Institute, Charles Murray was born and raised in Newton, Iowa. He obtained a degree in history from Harvard and a PhD from the Massachusetts Institute of Technology. He first came to prominence with his controversial book *Losing Ground* (1984) and co-authored (with Richard Hernstein) *The Bell Curve* (1994), the most successful criminology book of the 1990s in terms of sales. He has written widely on the underclass and is a leading advocate of imprisonment as an effective form of deterrence. His work has been heavily criticised by liberal and left-wing penologists.

Professor Andrew Rutherford (born 1940) Andrew Rutherford is Professor of Law and Criminal Policy at the University of Southampton. He was an undergraduate at Durham University (1961) and was awarded a Diploma in Criminology from Canterbury in 1962. From 1962 until 1973, he was an assistant and deputy governor in the Prison Service. One of the leading penal reductionists of recent years, Rutherford was chairman of the Howard League for Penal Reform between 1984–99. His main publications include *Prisons and the Process of Justice* (1984) and *Criminal Justice and the Pursuit of Decency* (1993).

Professor Joe Sim A leading member of the European Group for the Study of Deviance and Social Control and penal pressure group INQUEST, Joe Sim is one of the most influential penal campaigners and abolitionists of his generation. Currently Professor of Criminology at Liverpool John Moore University, he previously worked at the University of Stirling and for the Open University, at which he was awarded a PhD under the supervision of Professor Stuart Hall. Joe Sim has published a number of books, including *British Prisons* (with Michael Fitzgerald, first published in 1979), *Prisons Under Protest* (1991, with Phil Scraton and Paula Skidmore) and *The Carceral State* (2008). His book *Medical Power in Prisons* (1990) is widely regarded as one of most important works on imprisonment in the last three decades.

Penal expansionism and 'prison works'

Andrew Rutherford (1984) argued that 'penal expansion' is taking place when:

- prisoner populations are rising;
- prisons are overcrowded;
- the proposed solution is to build new prisons;
- there is an increase in numbers of prison staff;
- there is greater security across the penal estate.

In recent times, all of these factors have been evident in penal policy in England and Wales.

Average daily population (ADP) of prisoners in England and Wales every ten years from 1884–2004

- 1884   25,866
- 1894   17,127
- 1904   21,360
- 1914   15,743
- 1924   10,750
- 1934   12,238
- 1944   12,635
- 1954   22,421
- 1964   29,600
- 1974   36,867
- 1984   43,295
- 1994   48,621
- 2004   74,658

The figures in Figure 2.4 clearly indicate that the prison population in England and Wales has been rising since the 1940s. In 1940, the ADP was 9,377 prisoners; in 2007, the ADP stood at over 80,000 prisoners. In 2004, 116,000 people entered UK prisons and 186,000 people were sentenced to community punishments. Since 1974, the prison population has kept pace with rises in 'crime' rates and, in recent times, incarceration rates have gone well beyond the (falling) recorded 'crime' figures. Despite such sustained increases, there is nothing inevitable about growing prison populations.

Prison populations are political choices that are made by the government, by means of the laws it introduces and the subsequent interpretation of these laws by the judiciary. Most penologists have been very concerned about the massive rise in prison populations. But some politicians—such as Michael Howard, the Conservative Home Secretary in the 1990s—and other thinkers—such as Charles Murray, a right-wing American populist thinker—have argued that prisons work and that we should send more people to prison.

Charles Murray (1997) argues that, if used sufficiently, prison can work on the grounds of deterrence and incapacitation. Murray maintains that there is a clear link between the recorded 'crime' rate and imprisonment rates.

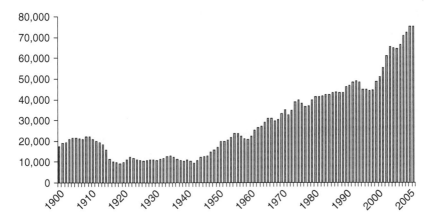

Figure 2.4   Prison statistics for England and Wales 1900–2005
Source: Newburn (2007)

Charles Murray (1997) argues that, from 1955–93, the risk of being sent to prison was cut by 80 per cent. Contrary to expectations, prisons have actually witnessed a period of great decline, largely due to the failings of prosecutors.

> **Common pitfall**   *Remember that official criminal statistics are social constructions that are there to serve the administration of the system. They are not hard or true facts that provide a comprehensive view of criminality and wrongdoing in a given society. Care should also be taken when analysing prison statistics.*

Murray suggests that the United Kingdom should '*reverse the great decline in imprisonment*' and that it should look to the USA for evidence that this can contain official 'crime'. Murray explains how, in 1974, there were 218,205 prisoners in the USA, but that the 'crime' rate was out of control; the massive increase in the use of custody, containing 2 million prisoners in 2000, has held the official 'crime' rate in check. When translated to England and Wales, Murray argues that, to reverse the decline in prison, the average daily population must reach 275,000 (over a quarter of a million) prisoners. Then, says Murray, we must keep the prison rate high, because that is the only way in which we can contain 'crime' rates. But even such a massive increase in imprisonment will not singularly reduce 'crime', because the real cause of 'crime' is welfare dependency.

Not very many penologists take the great decline argument seriously, but its simplicity may be seductive to politicians, some members of the public and even some penology students.

Prison does not work...

The criticisms made against Charles Murray (1997) include the following.

1. His analysis is overly simplistic and does not meet normal scholarly standards.
2. The 'crime' rate is a social construction and we cannot use this as an accurate measure of actual level of crimes.
3. 'Crime' and imprisonment rates fluctuate from country to country, and the relationship between 'crime' and punishment is very complex.
4. There is no evidence that prisons actually do deter.
5. Imprisonment creates more problems than it solves and may actually lead to increases in 'crime' rather than to its reduction.
6. If there is a lesson to be learnt from the US incarceration binge, it is that prisons do not work.

Penal standstill

The first alternative to penal expansionism is to attempt to keep the prison population at around its current population. In the mid–late 1980s, 'penal standstill' was the dominant rhetoric in official penal policy. Andrew Rutherford (1984, pp. 54–5) has identified the following aspects of penal standstill:

- exhortations by politicians to reduce custody;
- the development of non-custodial sanctions to replace imprisonment;
- a construction programme that is intended to replace existing prisons;
- greater discretion to reduce sentence length;
- a ceiling placed on ADP of prisoners;
- pragmatism and realism characterising the aims of imprisonment.

*It is easy to confuse **standstill** policies with penal **reductionism**.*

Penal reductionism

A large number of penologists have promoted 'penal reductionism'. These range from administrative penologies, which are often philosophically close to both the standstill and reductionist models, to more socialist-inspired penologies, which advocate radical agendas that are not that dissimilar to those of penal abolitionists.

> All penal reductionists share a commitment to decent prison conditions, the acknowledgement of prisoners' procedural and due process legal rights, and consider imprisonment to be merely a suspension of offender liberties. Following the famous dictum of Sir Alexander Paterson, one of the foremost prison administrators in the early part of the twentieth century, people are sent to prison as punishment, not for punishment.

Penal reductionists highlight how prison populations in England and Wales were drastically cut at the beginning of the twentieth century. In 1908, the throughput for prisons was 200,000, with an ADP of 22,029. By 1918, the ADP had dropped to 9,196 and, in 1938, the ADP was 11,086, with a throughput of less than 40,000. Through the promotion of genuine alternatives—such as probation, the abolishment of imprisonment for debt and allowing time for fines to be paid by offenders— the prison population was dramatically reduced. Underscoring this change was a political commitment to reducing prison numbers.

Although penal reductionists sometimes direct attention towards social problems, such as poverty or racism, reform of the criminal justice system has normally been their central focus. Penal reductionists raise concerns centring on:

- high prison populations;
- overcrowding;
- inadequate living conditions;
- culture of criminal justice staff;
- denial of prisoner legal rights.

Penal reductionists are often reluctant advocates of the prison, unable to conceive of responses to social harms that do not rely upon this 'detestable solution'. Penal reductionists call for:

- a reduction in the physical capacity of prisons to 20,000–40,000;
- imprisonment to be restricted for serious crimes only;

- legal enforced minimum standards;
- greater penal accountability;
- less punitive sentencing;
- the creation of more non-imprisonable offences;
- the early release of prisoners;
- development of alternatives to prison.

Prison populations are understood as political and policy choices. The aims of penal reform are to create greater scepticism about the benefits of prison and to muster the political will to change.

The limitations of penal reductionism include that it:

- is confined within a liberal political ideology that naturalises the prison;
- demonstrates no consideration of how imprisonment is intimately connected with structural divisions and definitions of social harms;
- does not question the power to punish and that reforms support the legitimacy of imprisonment;
- does not fully take into account the knowledge of prisoners.

There are a number of different approaches to penal reductionism. Although they are all largely arguing for similar things, there are often major inconsistencies and differences between theorists and how they advocate penal reforms. A classic example is the debate between Andrew Rutherford, and Roy King and Rod Morgan. Both camps are reductionists but King and Morgan (1980) argued for the principle of normalisation—that prison life should be as normal as possible—while Rutherford (1984) is highly critical of this, arguing that prisons can never be normal places.

Penal abolitionism

There are many similarities between penal reductionism and 'penal abolitionism'. The main difference is that abolitionists have questioned the role and function of the prison in advanced capitalist societies, and the actual necessity of human suffering through incarceration. Rene van Swaaningen argues that:

> at its core, criminal law ... is based on ... repressive assumptions ... From the beginning it has been seen to create problems instead of solving them. A penal reaction after the fact is not preventive but de-socialises an ever-increasing number of people. Therefore it would be better to abolish penal means of coercion, and to replace them by more reparative means. This briefly is the abolitionist message.

(1986, p. 9)

Abolitionists have been concerned with both the micro-realities of imprisonment, such as the lived experiences of prisoners, the inherent brutalities and dehumanisation of prison life, and the unfettered discretion of prison officers. Alongside this is a concern with the broader macro socio-economic contexts through which social harms are both understood and defined as 'crime', and which legitimises the current focus on, and indeed existence of, the process of penalisation.

Penal abolitionism has been criticised on the following grounds.

1 **Irresponsibility** It advocates releasing 'dangerous' prisoners and does not provide an agenda to protect victims or to deal with 'crimes' of the powerful.

2 **Irrelevance** It does not engage with current political debates and so does not help the powerless, because it is easily defined out of the debate.

3 **Idealism** It provides unrealistic, modernist visions of alternatives, which can be dangerous and rooted in left-wing 'fantasy'.

In fact, penal abolitionism does none of the above. Abolitionists generally promote responsible, relevant and realistic accounts of the penal system.

Responsibility

A responsible approach to wrongdoing must ask the following questions:

- do prisons help the victims of crime?
- do prisons help the offender or do they make the behaviour of the offender worse?
- do we imprison the people who cause the greatest harm?

Penal abolitionists can be seen to pursue the following goals in relation to as a responsible response to social harms.

1 **Justice for all** Our society is profoundly unequal, with major deficiencies surrounding social justice. What governments should do is look to provide justice, inclusion, integration, safety and security for all citizens, whether they are 'victims' or 'offenders'. This means doing something to address wrongdoing that actually works, rather than imprisonment, which generally makes the situation worse.

2 *The reduction of dehumanisation and unnecessary suffering*
Abolitionists fight against dehumanisation, unnecessary human suffering and the infringement of humanity, both inside and outside of the prison. They argue that suffering, pain and harm should be reduced wherever and whenever possible for all concerned, and believe that punishment (the intentional infliction of suffering) is largely an immoral act.

3 *Responsibilisation of the powerful* Our prisons are largely filled with poor, vulnerable, harmed, relatively powerless property offenders. Responsibilities should be tied to power and the actions of the powerful should be legally and democratically accountable.

Relevance

A relevant approach to penal policy today would ask:

- what are the implications of the current political climate for penal reform?
- what reforms do prisoners advocate?
- what is the most plausible and relevant form of struggle?

To this end, the following are critical factors.

1 *Reflexivity in a negative political climate* Current political reali- ties are shaped by the Thatcherite settlement, which prioritises neoliberal political economy, and under which governmental sover- eignty relies on a strong, potent and authoritarian state that can ensure security. This breeds a hostile social, economic and political context; in response, abolitionists have called for a moratorium on prison building and the protection of prisoner human rights.

2 *The need to legitimate the experiences of prisoners* Abolitionists root their legitimacy in the meanings that prisoners have given to their own lived reality. They have attempted to present a picture of real life: an accurate portrayal of the subjects' understandings, meanings and interpretations of the social world. Abolitionists have presented reforms that have accurately reflected the protests and resistance of the subjugated and the grass roots movements. The adoption of the 'view from below' opened up space in which abolition- ists could acknowledge and provide solidarity to prisoners. Contemporary abolitionists have, however, also retained some dis- tance to allow critical judgements of prisoner meanings that are rooted in discriminatory beliefs.

3 *Competing contradiction and human rights* Thomas Mathiesen (1974) argued that abolitionism must attain the '*competing contradiction*', because this was the only way to avoid being either co-opted by the state or being defined out as irrelevant. The 'competing contradiction' is competitive because it is relevant to the material conditions of the confined and a contradiction because it is in opposition to the broader goals of the penal system. Human rights, legal guarantees and positive (welfare) rights for citizens can achieve the competing contradiction, and have been central to recent abolitionist debates. In addition, prisoners have often understood their struggles against the brutalising nature of imprisonment through a human rights and legal framework.

Realism

A realistic approach to dealing with social problems would ask:

- do prisons reduce 'crime' or solve moral conflicts?
- do prisons really protect society?
- what alternatives work?

The penal abolitionist responds with the following.

1 *The punitive sanction really does not work* There will always be moral conflicts, but the term 'crime' should be replaced with alternative terms, such as 'problematic behaviours' or 'troublesome actions' that are understood in terms of harm. The criminal and penal law fail to solve problems or protect the vulnerable. They should not be used to regulate human interactions and so should be drastically reduced, or abolished.

2 *Law is an arena for resistance* Abolitionists recognise that the law is neither 'innocent' nor 'evil'; rather, the law is an arena of struggle and can lead to emancipation or repression. The rule of law is a means of protection and coercion, a mechanism for establishing democratic freedoms and legitimating terror. Abolitionists have selectively endorsed penal reforms. Their aim has been to challenge and exploit the contradictory nature of both the law and the state, and to bring about reforms that will have a positive impact on the concrete everyday existence of marginalised and excluded groups.

3 *A real commitment to justice and alternatives that really do work* A mandatory response is required for problems, conflicts

and wrongdoing, but the forms of redress do not necessarily have to involve the deliberate infliction of pain. Abolitionism is rooted in both deconstruction (critique) and reconstruction (alternatives). Abolitionist alternatives have ranged from promoting alternative ways of thinking that reject the punitive rationale, to concrete projects that look to work with offenders, to radical socialist political transformations that challenge the dominant forms of governmental sovereignty and political economy.

It is important that you consider all of the perspectives surrounding prisons and punishment. It is easy to construct a 'straw man', by failing to include all of the arguments surrounding a particular position, and then tear it down in what appears to be a compelling way—but penologists and practitioners will neither believe nor advocate positions that do not have some form of intellectual coherence. All published works should be taken on their merits. You should allow your imagination to take hold and try to think like a penologist. Look at prisons, from the perspective of right-wing, liberal and abolitionist standpoints: all three have their strengths and weaknesses, and you should explore them thoroughly.

Thinking critically about penal legitimacy

The claims of penal authorities to legitimacy are predicated upon the current distribution and application of punishment, and upon successfully attaining political validity and a sense of moral rightfulness in a given society, and lead to acquiescence, obedience and consent from both those imprisoned and from the general public. Failure to attain such moral or political validity can be assessed in two ways: as creating a legitimacy 'deficit' or as leading to a 'crisis' of penal legitimacy.

A prison service can be considered as suffering from a **legitimacy deficit** when the absence of legitimacy is believed to derive from weak justifications for its current aims, objectives and or stated purposes, if it appears to be inadequate in terms of fulfilling its desired goals and stated intentions, or if the authority of those who apply penal power is significantly undermined.

The current appliance of the power to punish can be considered to be illegitimate when it is claimed to create too many inherent infringements of human rights, when dehumanising penal regimes and brutalisation are considered to be endemic to operational practice, when it inevitably exceeds certain tolerable pain thresholds, or when it is believed to be entirely misapplied or that it inappropriately punishes certain categories of harm or wrongdoers. There are subsequently two dimensions to this *'crisis of penal legitimacy'* (Fitzgerald and Sim, 1982):

* political legitimacy;
* moral legitimacy.

Fitzgerald and Sim provide a classic statement of the crisis of *political* legitimacy:

> the sanction of imprisonment is invoked consistently against marginal, lower class offenders. In so doing, imprisonment serves a class-based legal system, which first, defines the social harm which are signalled out for punishment, and second, invokes different types of sanctions for different categories of social harm.
>
> (1982, p. 24)

For abolitionists such as Joe Sim, imprisonment cannot be understood outside of social context—i.e. the social divisions and structural inequities of society around racism, sexism and poverty. Because we lock up the poor, the vulnerable and the powerless, rather than the most dangerous, prisons do not do what they claim to do. In this sense, they are politically illegitimate.

The *moral* legitimacy of imprisonment has also been questioned. For Barbara Hudson and a number of abolitionists from Continental Europe, imprisonment must be understood within the wider debates on punishment (the intentional imposition of suffering). The very deployment of the punitive rationale and punishment itself, rather than the liberal reductionist concerns with prison conditions or standards, become the central focus of a moral critique. For many abolitionists, the deliberate infliction of pain is inherently morally problematic and so the penal system also faces a crisis of moral legitimacy.

The term 'neo-abolitionism' was first introduced by Dutch abolitionist Rene van Swaaningen. Some neo-abolitionists (Scott, 2006) argue that prisons are profoundly immoral and represent the negation of humanity, on the bases that:

* the label 'prisoner' constructs a dehumansing context;
* the pains of imprisonment are structured, and present inherent threats to human dignity and respect;
* prisons are a spatial matrix that is predicated on violence and legalised terror;
* prisons dehabilitate people.

The prison is an inherently harm-creating environment that has direct implications for the health of those confined. For anti-prison critics, penal institutions are detestable solutions that we can live without—and this implies their deligitimation.

Neo-abolitionists point to the crises of both moral and political legitimacy.

Radical alternatives

Radical alternatives to prison have taken three forms, as follows.

- **Political** The promotion of norm-creating social policies that are rooted in social justice (recognition and respect as fellow humans, and the equitable redistribution of wealth), democratic accountability and human rights.
- **Cognitive** A new way of thinking about social problems that is focused on redress, reparation and restoration in relation to harm done.
- **Practical** Concrete alternatives that include offenders and attempt to address offenders' needs. These can be preventative—such as providing investment into youth clubs, constructive employment opportunities and social inclusion— or through promoting restorative justice and community activities that empower, improve skills, meet needs and invest in offenders as human beings.

"Are abolitionist perspectives plausible in a time of penal expansionism?"

First, you need to explain what you mean by both 'penal abolitionism' and 'penal expansionism'. Discuss, then, the main themes of the abolitionist perspectives. Highlight the criticisms made against abolitionism, paying particular attention to current political realities and the impact of abolitionism upon penal policies. You may wish to conclude with a defence of abolitionism, looking at its use of reflexivity, and more limited goals and aims, such as the promotion of prisoner human rights.

 Taking it **FURTHER**

There are a number of different penal reductionist perspectives. Below are detailed six different approaches.

Six approaches to penal reductionism	Key thinkers
The Cambridge School	Alison Liebling (2004) *Prisons and their Moral Performance*
Fabian socialists	Vivien Stern (1989) *Imprisoned by Our Prisons*
Left realist	Roger Matthews (1999) *Doing Time*
Normalisation	Roy King and Rod Morgan (1980) *The Future of the Prison*
Radical liberal	Andrew Rutherford (1984) *Prisons and the Process of Justice*
Radical pluralists (Weberian)	Michael Cavadino and James Dignan (2007) *The Penal System,* 4th edn

Textbook guide

CAVADINO, M AND DIGNAN, J (2007) *The Penal System,* 4th edn, London: Sage

FITZGERALD, M AND SIM, J (1982) *British Prisons,* 2nd edn, Oxford: Blackwell

JEWKES, Y (2007) *Handbook of Prisons,* Cullompton: Willan Publishing

MATTHEWS, R (1999) *Doing Time,* London: Palgrave

RUTHERFORD, A (1984) *Prisons and the Process of Justice,* Oxford: Oxford University Press

RYAN, M (2005) *Penal Policy and Political Culture,* Winchester: Waterside Press

VAN SWAANINGEN, R (1997) *Critical Criminology: Visions from Europe,* London: Sage

part three*

study, writing and revision skills

Core areas: **3.1 how to get the most out of your lectures and seminars**

3.2 writing a dissertation

3.3 essay-writing hints

3.4 revision hints

3.5 exam hints

*in collaboration with David McIlroy

3.1

how to get the most out of your lectures and seminars

Core areas: **use of lecture notes**
mastering technical terms
developing independent study
note-taking strategy
developing the lecture
seminars should not be underestimated

It is the responsibility of your tutors to provide module booklets detailing lecture topics, seminar questions and recommended readings. It is a good idea to become familiar with your module outlines as soon as possible. Before you go into each lecture, you should briefly remind yourself of where it fits into the overall scheme of things.

It is a good idea to purchase the main recommended textbooks before the start of the module. If you act early, and read through the lecture and seminar programme, you may be able to pick up further supplementary texts second-hand from the university bookshop.

Use of lecture notes

It is always beneficial to do some preliminary reading before you enter a lecture. If lecture notes are provided in advance (e.g. electronically), then read these over and bring them with you to the lecture. Some lecturers prefer to provide full notes; some prefer to make skeletal outlines available; and some prefer not to issue notes at all. If notes are provided, take full advantage and supplement these with your own notes as you listen. Some basic preparation will equip you with a great advantage: you will be able to 'tune in' and think more clearly about the lecture than you would have been able to had you not undertaken the preliminary work.

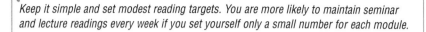

Keep it simple and set modest reading targets. You are more likely to maintain seminar and lecture readings every week if you set yourself only a small number for each module.

Mastering technical terms

New words can be threatening, especially if you have to face a string of them in one lecture. Uncertainty about new terms may impair your ability to benefit fully from the lecture and may therefore hinder the quality of your learning. Some subjects require technical terms and the use of them is unavoidable—but when you have heard a term a number of times, it will not seem as daunting as it did initially.

Checklist for mastering terms used in your lectures

✓   Read lecture notes before the lectures.

✓   List any unfamiliar terms.

✓   Read over the listed terms until you are familiar with their sound.

✓   Try to work out meanings of terms from their context.

✓   Do not suspend learning the meaning of a term indefinitely.

✓   Write out a sentence that includes the new word (do this for each word).

✓   Meet with other students and test each other with the technical terms.

✓   Jot down new words you hear in lectures and check out their meaning soon afterwards.

Your confidence will greatly increase when you begin to follow the flow of arguments that contain technical terms, especially when you can freely use the terms yourself, both in speaking and writing.

Developing independent study

Lectures are signposts for further reading. The issues raised in your lectures are designed to help you and to inspire you to undertake deeper independent study. Your aim should invariably be to build on what you are given and you should never merely return the bare bones of the lecture material in a piece of coursework or in an exam.

It is always very refreshing for a lecturer or examiner to receive assignments or exam answers that contain references to recent studies that he or she has not highlighted in a related lecture or has not previously encountered.

Note-taking strategy

Note taking in lectures is an art that you will only perfect with practice, and by trial and error. The problem will always be to try to find a balance between concentrating on what you hear, and making sufficient notes that will enable you later to remember and reflect on what you have heard. You should not, however, become frustrated by the fact that you will not immediately understand or remember everything that you have heard.

By being present at a lecture and by making some attempt to make notes on what you hear, you will already have a substantial advantage over those students who do not even attend.

Guidelines for note taking in lectures

To develop a note-taking strategy that works best for you, work at finding a balance between listening and writing. This may entail listing a few key words to summarise the issues discussed in the lecture. Do, however, remember the following points.

- Too much writing may impair the flow of the lecture for you.
- Too much writing may impair the quality of your notes.
- Some limited notes are better than none.
- Good note taking may facilitate deeper processing of information.
- It is essential to 'tidy up' notes as soon as possible after a lecture.
- Reading over notes soon after lectures will consolidate your learning.

Developing the lecture

Lectures are sometimes criticised as a form of 'passive learning'. Some lecturers, however, make their lectures more interactive, by using interactive handouts or by posing questions during the lecture and giving students time out to reflect on these. As a student, you can also make the lecture more interactive in the following ways.

✓ Try to interact with the lecture material by asking questions.
✓ Highlight points that you would like to develop in personal study.
✓ Trace connections between the lecture and other parts of your study programme.
✓ Bring together notes from the lecture and other sources.
✓ Restructure the lecture outline into your own preferred format.
✓ Think of ways in which aspects of the lecture material can be applied.
✓ Design ways in which aspects of the lecture material can be illustrated.
✓ If the lecturer invites questions, make a note of all of the questions asked.
✓ Follow up on issues of interest that have arisen out of the lecture.

Seminars should not be underestimated

Seminars are often optional in a degree programme and are sometimes poorly attended, because they are underestimated. But seminars have a unique contribution to learning that will complement lectures. Seminars can:

✓ identify problems of which you had not previously thought;
✓ clear up confusing issues;
✓ allow you to ask questions and make comments;
✓ help you to develop friendships and teamwork;
✓ enable you to refresh and consolidate your knowledge;
✓ help you to sharpen your motivation and to redirect your study efforts.

Strategies for benefiting from your seminar experience

There are a number of ways in which you can benefit from seminars.

✓ Do some preparatory reading.
✓ Familiarise yourself with the main ideas to be addressed.
✓ Make notes during the seminar.

✓ Make some verbal contribution, even if it is only a single question.

✓ Remind yourself of the skills that you can develop.

✓ Trace learning links from the seminar to other topics on your programme.

✓ Make brief bullet points relating to on what you should follow up.

✓ Read over your notes as soon as possible after the seminar.

✓ Continue discussion with fellow students after the seminar has ended.

If you are required to give a presentation as part of your seminar, the following points will be helpful.

- Have a practice run with friends.
- If using visuals, do not obstruct them.
- Check out beforehand that all equipment works.
- Space out your points clearly on any visuals (i.e. make them large and legible).
- Time your presentation in relation to your visuals (e.g. five slides for a 15-minute talk = 3 minutes per slide).
- Make sure that your presentation synchronises with the slide on view at any given point.
- Project your voice so that all in the room can hear.
- Inflect your voice and do not stand motionless.
- Spread eye contact around the audience.
- Avoid the twin extremes of a fixed gaze on certain individuals or of never looking at anyone.
- It is better to fall a little short of time allocated than to run over.
- Be selective in what you choose to present.
- Map out where you are going and summarise your main points at the end.

3.2	
writing a dissertation	

Core areas: **the research process**
preparation and focus
chapter structure
supervision
from first thoughts to final draft

The research process

A dissertation is an independent piece of work that you will be expected to do, probably in the third year of your undergraduate degree or towards the end of a taught postgraduate degree. The length of your dissertation can range from 8,000 to 20,000 words. If you are doing a research degree, the word length will be even longer. Undergraduate dissertations are normally 10,000 words. Although this may sound a lot at the start, by the time at which you come to submit your dissertation, you will probably wish it could be much longer. The art of writing a dissertation is to keep to the word limit and to cover the issues that need to be incorporated into your work. This is often the hardest part, and so it is important that you give the topic, focus, structure and availability of literature a great deal of thought. It will be down to you to identify the focus of your studies, to set deadlines, to arrange supervision times, to organise chapter structures and to undertake a literature review

> It is important, in a large project (such as a dissertation), that you choose a topic for which you can maintain your motivation, momentum and enthusiasm.

Preparation and focus

It is sensible, if you are doing a dissertation on prisons or punishment, that you have undertaken the relevant modules. This will give you an overview of the general literature, help you to focus on one specific area and assist with your background reading. You will need to convince your supervisor that there is enough material easily available for you to undertake the project. Always start with the most broad and straightforward books, and then work your way into the specialist area.

> Time is also very important. If you are an undergraduate student, you should start thinking about your dissertation in your second year; as a postgraduate on a taught course, it is worthwhile thinking about your dissertation as soon as you start your course.

Undergraduate students should probably undertake literature reviews rather than empirical research. This is because doing empirical work well is quite difficult, and there are also clear ethical issues that need to be addressed in the design and application of the dissertation. If you are a postgraduate students you may consider doing empirical research, especially if you have had research training or have developed transferable skills through your work. Focus is all-important. You should ask yourself what exactly you want to examine in your dissertation: a common mistake is to try to do too much. This is natural and you will probably find that, as you progress with your project, you will refine the topic to a much smaller issue, or group of issues. Once you have established a clear focus, a good structure is the key to success.

Chapter structure

Once you have some idea which aspect of penology you wish to investigate and have decided on a central question or focus, you need to think about chapter structure. This may involve some background reading into how best to write and present your dissertation. It is always important that you speak to your supervisor about chapter structure, but a penology dissertation might be organised in the following way, with proportionate word counts:

1 ***Introduction to study and context to research question*** (Word count: 5–10%)

- What is the focus of your study?
- How can the research issue be understood in context?
- What theoretical position have you adopted?
- What is the structure and content of the following chapters?

2 ***Definitions, data and historical contexts*** *(Word count: 15–20%)*

- What are the major historical developments?
- What is the official definition and data on the given issue?
- Should these social constructions be problematised?

3 ***Theories and explanations*** *(Word count: 15–20%)*

- What are the dominant ways of thinking about the issue?
- Are there competing explanations?
- What approach are you taking?

4 ***Policy*** *(Word count: 15–20%)*

- What are the main penal polices on this issue?
- What are their strengths and weaknesses?

5 Case studies *(Word count: 15–20%)*

- What are the main cases linked to your research focus?
- What do problems, concerns or good practices highlight?

6 Evaluation of case studies/effectiveness of current responses *(Word count: 15–20%)*

- How does the case study link to the main research question?
- How is a given problem investigated or examined by the government?

7 Conclusion *(Word count: less than 5%)*

- How have you answered the research question or explored the topic focus?
- What are the implications of your findings?

> *When working out your chapter structure, you should be looking to provide a platform for the central focus of the dissertation. Chapters should be building blocks that are leading the reader towards a case study or empirical evidence.*

In many dissertations, your evaluation and conclusion can be combined into one chapter. This will allow you a greater percentage of the word count in the preceding chapters. If you are doing empirical research instead of a literature review, you will need to provide a methodology chapter. Every dissertation is different, so you may wish to deviate from this structure in a number of ways. Your supervisor will be well placed to help you to organise your chapters and to help you to focus on your dissertation topic.

Self-inflicted deaths in prison

Example question and research focus: 'How many people die in custody, who is to blame, and who is held to account?'

- *Introduction* Outline of chapter structure and context of the dissertation— for example, rates of self-inflicted deaths in the community, rising prison populations, or human rights issues.
- *Chapter 1* Definitions and data of self-inflicted deaths in prison—you might identify the social and historical constructions of data, and discuss age, 'race', gender and other differentials in official rates.

(Continued)

- *Chapter 2* Overview of different theories and explanations of deaths in prison, highlighting the allocation of blame.
- *Chapter 3* Critical appraisal of the policies of the government and Prison Service responses, such as the introduction of Assessment, Care in Custody and Teamwork (ACCT).
- *Chapter 4* Case studies of recent high-profile self-inflicted deaths in prison—ensure that the cases you choose are the subject of sufficient literature that you are able to write a substantial amount on each case.
- *Chapter 5* Analysis of official investigations into self-inflicted deaths and forms of accountability.
- *Conclusion* Answer the specific question you have asked and identified as the central focus of the dissertation—what does this tell us about penal legitimacy?

Supervision

Supervision is very important. Supervisors provide intellectual support, but can also help you with basic referencing and layout tips. In addition, the research process is rather lonely and your supervisor should share an interest in the topic you are studying, therefore providing support. In the first or second meeting with your supervisor, you should be able to offer:

- a clear topic area;
- a specific focus or question;
- a list of references that you can access, having already undertaken a small amount of reading;
- an idea of how you are going to structure your dissertation chapters;
- the deadlines of when you are going to submit your chapters.

Do not be afraid to ask or approach a potential supervisor in the first instance—you want to be supervised by somebody who is an expert in the area and who can help you with your focus and structure.

It is the responsibility of the supervisor to ensure that he or she is available to see you over the year, but it is down to you to make sure that you use that time constructively. This means having something new for your supervisor to read and also giving him or her plenty of time to read drafts before meetings. Emailing chapters an hour before a supervisory meeting is unlikely to leave your supervisor in the most favourable of moods!

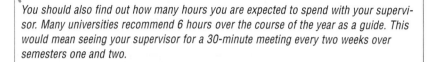

> You should also find out how many hours you are expected to spend with your supervisor. Many universities recommend 6 hours over the course of the year as a guide. This would mean seeing your supervisor for a 30-minute meeting every two weeks over semesters one and two.

From first thoughts to final draft

Motivation is very important when undertaking research. You must be interested in the topic and prepared to work hard. A well-organised dissertation should be fun to do and should allow you to gather specialist knowledge in penology. Completing the first draft of the dissertation is the hardest part. You should always try to finish your dissertation with a few weeks to spare. This will allow you to proofread your dissertation and spot any small mistakes or contradictory arguments. When reading a dissertation, you should initially focus on the content, rather than on sentence structure or referencing problems. Everything takes longer than you think: you may expect to finish a chapter in a couple of weeks, but it will probably take twice as long. When writing, remember that you should write as an academic, and that you must be able to explain and apply all of the concepts that you use. Name dropping may be useful in exams, but will not help you much with your dissertation. Write in a clear and understandable way and explain what you mean. Do not take the reader's knowledge for granted. You are being tested on what you know and how you came to these conclusions, rather than on the fact that you have picked up a couple of key words or concepts.

> The hard work will pay off: rewrites, especially if you follow the guidance of your dissertation supervisor, will lead to better marks. Remember that your supervisor is also likely to be one of your markers.

Checklist for your dissertation

✓ Give yourself as much time as possible to work on your topic.
✓ Ensure that you undertake background reading and that enough material is available.

✓   Have a clear focus and structure.

✓   Set yourself deadlines from the beginning.

✓   Make sure that you make the most of your supervision.

✓   Complete a first draft at least a month before the deadline.

✓   Ensure that the final draft has been proofread and is properly referenced.

3.3	
essay-writing hints	

Core areas: **getting into the flow**

the 'tributary' principle

listing and linking the key concepts

addressing penal controversies

structuring an outline

identifying key questions

rest your case

careful use of quotations

a clearly defined 'Introduction'

the 'Conclusion': adding the finishing touches

top-down and bottom-up clarity

Getting into the flow

When writing an essay (or dissertation chapter), one of your first aims should be to get your mind active and engaged with your subject. It is a good idea to 'warm up' for your essay by jotting down key themes and ideas before you begin to write. This will allow you to think within the framework of your topic and will be especially important if you are coming to the subject for the first time.

The 'tributary' principle

A 'tributary' is a stream that runs into a main river as it wends its way to the sea. Similarly, in an essay, you should ensure that every idea you introduce is moving towards the overall theme you are addressing. Your idea might, of course, be relevant to a subheading that is, in turn, relevant to a main heading. Every idea you introduce is to be a 'feeder' into the flowing theme.

In addition to tributaries, there can also be 'distributaries', which are streams that flow away from the river. In an essay, these would represent the ideas that run away from the main stream of thought and leave the reader trying to work out what their relevance may have been. It is one thing to have grasped your subject thoroughly, but quite another to convince your reader that this is the case. Your aim should be to build up ideas sentence by sentence and paragraph by paragraph, until you have communicated your clear purpose to the reader.

> It is important, in essay writing, that you do not include irrelevant material and that you stay focused on the essay question. You can make linking statements that show a wider understanding of the issues, but you must ensure that you explain how they contribute to your answer and why you consider them to be relevant.

Listing and linking the key concepts

All subjects will have central concepts that can sometimes be usefully labelled by a single word. Course textbooks may include a glossary of terms and these provide a direct route to the beginning of efficient mastery of the topic. The central words or terms are the essential raw materials upon which you will need to build. Ensure that you learn the words and their definitions, and that you can go on to link the key words together so that, in your learning activities, you will add understanding to your basic memory work.

EXAMPLE: 'Write an essay answering the question "Are our prisons accountable?"'

You might decide to draft your outline points in the manner shown in Figure 3.1 (or you may prefer to use a mind map approach).

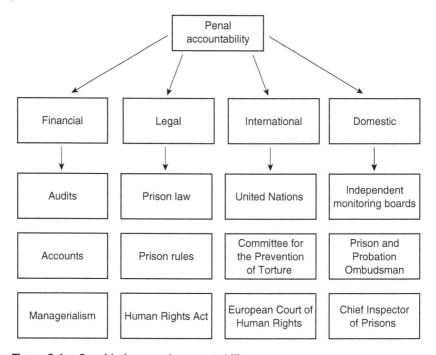

Figure 3.1   Considering penal accountability

Addressing penal controversies

In higher education, students are required to make the transition from descriptive to critical writing. You should imagine the critical approach to be like a law case that is being conducted, in which there is both a prosecution and a defence. Your concern should be for objectivity, transparency and fairness. No matter how passionately you may feel about a given cause, you must not allow information to be filtered out because of your personal prejudice. An essay is not to become a crusade for a cause in which the contrary arguments are not addressed in an even-handed manner. This means that you should show awareness that opposite views are held and these should be represented as accurately as possible. The above points do not, of course, mean that you are not entitled to a personal persuasion, or to feel passionately about your subject. On the contrary, such feelings may well be a marked advantage if you can bring them under control and channel them into balanced, effective writing.

EXAMPLE   of a controversial issue that may stir up passions: 'Offer arguments for and against the imprisonment of women offenders'

For

- 'Women offenders have broken the law and should be punished.'
- 'Society should be protected from dangerous women offenders.'
- 'To treat women differently would imply gender bias and discriminate against male offenders.'
- 'Women offenders are more abnormal or 'evil' than male offenders.'
- 'Women offenders are likely to suffer from a psychiatric illness.'
- 'Prison may provide an opportunity for women to be rehabilitated.'
- 'The punishment of women fits society's current punitive political ethos.'

Against

- 'Women offenders come from very impoverished social backgrounds.'
- 'Women offenders are likely to have been harmed by adult males.'
- 'Women have committed minor offences and are not dangerous.'
- 'Women experience different and more intense pains of imprisonment.'
- 'Prisons were designed to deal with men rather than women.'
- 'Prisons have largely failed to rehabilitate women.'
- 'The social consequences of imprisoning women are severe, especially for children and families.'

Structuring an outline

Whenever you sense a flow of inspiration to write on a given subject, it is essential that you put this into a structure that will allow your inspiration to be communicated clearly. It is a basic principle in all walks of life that structure and order facilitate good communication. Therefore, when you have the flow of inspiration in your essay, you must structure this in a way that will allow the marker to recognise the true quality of your work. For example, you might plan for an 'Introduction', a 'Conclusion' and three main sections, each with several subheadings (see example below). Moreover, you may decide not to include your headings in your final presentation—i.e. you may use them only initially to structure and balance your arguments. Once you have drafted this outline, you can then easily sketch an 'Introduction' and you will have been well prepared for the 'Conclusion' when you arrive at that point.

A good structure will help you to balance the weight of each of your arguments against the others and to arrange your points in the order that will best facilitate the fluent progression of your argument.

EXAMPLE: **'Write an essay answering the question "Does prison work?"'**

1 *What do we mean by the term 'prison works'?*

(i) Define what the term 'prison works' means and link to debates on deterrence and incapacitation.
(ii) Outline the political context and rise of the 'prison works' movement in the 1990s.
(iii) Highlight the main advocates of this perspective in the United Kingdom, such as Michael Howard.

2 *The implications of the 'prison works' agenda: penal expansionism*

(i) Provide the definition of 'penal expansionism' provided by Andrew Rutherford (1984).
(ii) Examine recent data on prison populations to assess the extent of penal expansionism.

3 *The defence of this perspective*

(i) Investigate the main arguments defending 'prison works', such as those of Charles Murray and the pressure group Civitas.
(ii) Overview the claims made regarding the relationship between 'crime' rates and levels of imprisonment.

4 *What criticisms can be made against this argument?*

(i) Consider the accuracy of the data deployed to defend rising rates of imprisonment.
(ii) Detail the philosophical evidence concerning deterrence and incapacitation.

Identifying key questions

When you are constructing a draft outline for an essay or project, you should ask what are the major questions that you wish to address. It is useful to make a list of all the issues that you might wish to tackle that spring to mind. The ability to design a good question is an art form that should be cultivated and such questions will allow you to impress your assessor with the quality of your thinking. To illustrate the point, consider the example presented below. If you were asked to write an essay about the real levels of violence in prison, you might, as your starting point, pose the following questions.

EXAMPLE: **'What are the real levels of violence in prison?'**

- What is the working definition of 'violence in prison' to be operationalised in the study?
- Where, when and how does violence occur in prison?
- Do officers turn a blind eye to prisoner-on-prisoner violence to help to facilitate the daily running of the prison?
- Do officers cover up violence perpetrated by other officers on prisoners?
- What are the levels of violence and intimidation that are experienced by officers?
- Do prisoners perceive the prison as 'safe'?
- Who investigates, collates and records data on violent incidents?
- Does the prison have an effective complaints procedure to deal with violent incidents?
- Do recent Prison Service statistics show increases or decreases in levels of violence in prison?
- Can we conclude that the official data is a fair reflection of reality? Why, or why not?
- Is violence inherent to the very nature of imprisonment?

Rest your case

It should be your aim to give the clear impression that your arguments are not based entirely on hunches, bias, feelings or intuition. In exams and essay questions, it is usually assumed (even if not directly specified) that you will appeal to evidence to support your claims. Therefore, when you write your essay or dissertation, you should ensure that it is liberally sprinkled with citations and evidence. By the time the assessor reaches the end of your work, he or she should be convinced that your conclusions are evidence-based. A fatal flaw would be to make claims for which you have provided no authoritative source.

Give the clear impression that what you have asserted is derived from recognised sources and is up to date. It also looks impressive if you spread your citations across your essay, rather than compressing them into a paragraph or two at the beginning and end.

Some examples of how you might introduce your evidence and sources are as follows.

- 'According to Liebling (2004) ...'
- 'Sim (2008) has concluded that ...'
- 'Cohen (2001) found that ...
- 'It has been claimed by Garland (1990) that ...'
- 'Hudson (2003) asserted that ...'
- 'A review of the evidence by Codd (2008) suggests that ...'

Careful use of quotations

Although it is desirable to present a good range of cited sources, it is not judicious to present these as 'patchwork quilt'—i.e. you should not simply paste together what others have said, with little thought for interpretative comment or coherent structure. It is a good general point to aim to avoid very lengthy extracts: short ones can be very effective. Aim to blend the quotations as naturally as possible into the flow of your sentences. Also, it is good to vary your practices: sometimes, you might use short, direct, brief quotations (citing page number, as well as author and year); at other times, you can summarise the gist of a quotation in your own words. In this latter case, you should cite the author's name and year of publication, but leave out quotation marks and page number.

A good guide for deciding whether to include a quotation is to consider if its author is a great authority in the field and so adds weight to your argument, or if you find the prose so beautifully or powerfully written that you could not hope to put it better yourself.

In terms of referencing, practice may vary from one discipline to the next, but some general points that will go a long way in contributing to good practice are:

- names and dates in text should correspond exactly with those listed in the 'References' or 'Bibliography';
- the list of 'References' and 'Bibliography' should be in alphabetical order by the surname (not the initials) of the author or first author;
- any reference you make in the text should be traceable by the reader (i.e. he or she should clearly be able to identify and trace the source).

A clearly defined 'Introduction'

In an 'Introduction' to an essay, you have the opportunity to define the problem or issue that is being addressed and to set it within context. Resist the temptation to elaborate on any issue at the introductory stage. The introduction should provide little tasters of what will follow, in order to whet the reader's appetite and to mark out the boundaries of your discussion.

> *If you leave the introduction and definition of your problem until the end of your writing, you will be better placed to map out the directions taken.*

The 'Conclusion': adding the finishing touches

In the 'Conclusion', you should aim to tie your essay together in a clear and coherent manner. It is your last chance to leave an overall impression in your reader's mind. Therefore, you will, at this stage, want to do justice to your efforts and not sell yourself short. This is your opportunity to identify what the strongest evidence points or where the balance of probability lies. The conclusion to an exam question often has to be written hurriedly under the pressure of time, but, with an essay or dissertation, you have time to reflect on, refine and adjust the content to your satisfaction. It should be your goal to make the conclusion a smooth finish that does justice to your range of content in summary and succinct form. Do not underestimate the value of an effective conclusion. 'Sign off' your essay in a manner that brings closure to the treatment of your subject.

Top-down and bottom-up clarity

An essay gives you the opportunity to refine each sentence and paragraph, remembering the 'tributary' principle. From a 'top-down' perspective—i.e. that of starting at the top with your major outline points—clarity is facilitated by the structure drafted in your outline. You can ensure that the subheadings are appropriately placed under the most relevant main heading, and that both subheadings and main headings are arranged in logical sequence. From a 'bottom-up' perspective—i.e. that of building up the details that 'flesh out' your main points—you should check that each sentence is a 'feeder' for the predominant concept in a given paragraph. When all of this is done, you can check that the transition from one point to the next is smooth, rather than abrupt.

Checklist: summary for essay writing

✓ Before you start, 'warm up' by giving yourself some thinking time.

✓ List the major concepts and link them in fluent form.

✓ Design a structure (outline) that will facilitate balance, progression, fluency and clarity.

✓ Pose questions and address these in a critical way.

✓ Demonstrate that your arguments rest on evidence and spread cited sources across your essay.

✓ Provide an 'Introduction' that sets the scene and a 'Conclusion' that rounds off the arguments.

3.4	
revision hints	

Core areas: **compile summary notes**
keep organised records
use past papers
employ effective memory aids
alternate between methods
revise with others

Strategy for revision should be on your mind from your very first lecture at the beginning of your academic semester. You should be like the squirrel that stores up nuts for the winter: do not waste any lecture, tutorial, seminar, group discussion, etc. by letting the material evaporate into thin air; get into the habit of making a few guidelines for revision after each learning activity. Keep a folder, file or small notebook that is reserved for revision and write out the major points that you have learned from each session. By establishing this regular practice, you will find that what you have learned becomes consolidated in your mind, and that this enables you to 'import' and 'export' your material both within and across subjects.

If you do this regularly and do not make the task too tedious, you will be amazed at how much useful summary material you have accumulated when it comes to revision time.

Compile summary notes

It would be useful and convenient to have a small notebook or cards on which you can write outline summaries that provide you with an overview of your subject at a glance. You might also use treasury tags to hold different batches of cards together, while still allowing for inserts and resorting. Such practical resources can easily be slipped into your pocket or bag and produced when you are on the bus or train, or while you are sitting in a traffic jam. A glance over your notes will consolidate your learning and will also encourage you to think further about your subject. It is also useful to make a note of questions that you would like to explore in greater depth at a later time.

There is a part of the mind that will continue to work on problems when you have moved on to focus on other issues. Therefore, if you feed on useful, targeted informa-tion, your mind will continue to work on 'automatic pilot' after you have 'switched off'.

Keep organised records

People who have a fulfilled career have usually developed the twin skills of time and task management. It is worth pausing to remember that you can use your academic training to prepare for your future career in this respect. You should ensure that you do not fall short of your potential simply because these qualities have not been cultivated.

One important tactic is to keep a folder for each subject and to divide this topic by topic, keeping your topics in the same order in which they are presented in your course lectures. Bind them together using subject dividers to separate the topics. At the front of the folder, compile an index of the contents, listing each topic clearly as a way of identifying each new section. Another important practice is to place all of your notes on a given topic within the appropriate section—and not to put off this simple task, but to do it straight away. Notes may come from lectures, seminars, tutorials, Internet searches, personal notes, etc. It is also essential that, when you remove these for consultation, you return them to their 'home' immediately after use.

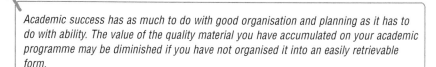

Academic success has as much to do with good organisation and planning as it has to do with ability. The value of the quality material you have accumulated on your academic programme may be diminished if you have not organised it into an easily retrievable form.

Use past papers

Revision will be very limited if it is confined to memory work. While you should read over your revision cards or notebook and keep a picture of the major facts in your mind's eye, it is also essential that you become familiar with previous exam papers to give you some idea of how the questions are likely to be framed. You can build up a good range of past exam papers (especially recent ones) and add these to your folder.

Employ effective memory aids

You should try to use devices that will help you to recall information that might otherwise be difficult to retrieve from memory. 'Visualisation' is one technique that can be used to aid memory: for example, the 'location method' involves you visualising a familiar journey and 'placing' the facts that you wish to remember at various landmarks along the journey—e.g. a bus stop, a car park, a shop, a store, a bend, a police station, a traffic light, etc. This has the advantage of associating the information that you have to learn with other material that is already firmly embedded and structured in your memory. Therefore, once the relevant memory is activated, a dynamic 'domino effect' will be triggered. There is, however, no reason why you cannot use a whole toolkit of memory aids.

Memory aids

Memory can be enhanced when information is processed in a range of modalities, such as hearing, seeing, speaking and visualising. Some examples are as follows.

- *Alliteration's artful aid* Phrase a key learning point in such a way that it forms a series of words that all begin with the same letter.
- The *'peg' system* 'Hang' information onto a term (an 'umbrella' term) so that, when you hear that term, you will remember the ideas connected with it.
- *Acronyms* Take the first letter of all of the key words and make a word from these. These are widely used in penology. Recent examples include NOMS—the National Offender Management Service—and CARATS—the Counselling, Advice, Referral, Assessment and Throughcare Services.
- *Mind maps* These allow you to draw lines that stretch out from the central idea to develop the subsidiary ideas in the same way.
- *'Rhymes and chimes'* Associate words that rhyme and words that end with a similar sound (e.g. criminalisation, penalisation, incarceration).

Alternate between methods

It is not enough, however, merely to present a list of outline points in response to an exam question (although it is better to do this than to do nothing if you have run out of time in your exam). Your aim should be to put 'meat on the bones', adding substance, evidence and arguments to your basic points. You should work at finding the balance between the two methods—outline revision cards might be best reserved for short bus journeys, whereas extended reading might be better employed for longer revision slots at home or in the library. Your ultimate goal should be to bring together an effective working approach that will enable you to face your exam questions comprehensively and confidently.

Revise with others

If you can find a few other students with whom to revise, this will provide another fresh approach to the last stages of your learning. First, ensure that others carry their own workloads and that they are not merely using the hard work of others as a short cut to success. You should think of group sessions as one of the strings on your violin, but not the only string. This collective approach will allow you to assess your strengths and weaknesses (showing you where you are offtrack), and to benefit from the resources and insights of others. Before you meet up, you can each design some questions for the whole group to address. The group might also go through past exam papers and discuss the points that might provide an effective response to each question— but it should not be the aim of the group to provide standard and identical answers that each group member can mimic. Group work is currently deemed to be advantageous by educationalists, and teamwork is held to be a desirable employability quality.

Checklist: good study habits for revision time

✓ Set a date for the 'official' beginning of revision and prepare for 'revision mode'.

✓ Do not force cramming by leaving revision too late.

✓ Take breaks from revision to avoid saturation.

✓ Indulge in relaxing activities to give your mind a break from pressure.

✓ Minimise or eliminate the use of alcohol during the revision season.

✓ Get into a good rhythm of sleep to allow for the renewal of your mind.

✓ Avoid excessive caffeine, especially at night, so that sleep is not disrupted.

✓ Try to adhere to regular eating patterns.

✓ Try to have a brisk walk in fresh air each day (e.g. in the park).

✓ Avoid excessive dependence on junk food and snacks.

3.5	
exam hints	

Core areas: **handling your nerves**
              time management
              task management
              attend to practical details

the art of 'name dropping'

a politician's answer

missing your question

pursue a critical approach

analyse the parts

when asked to 'discuss'

if a 'critique' is requested

if asked to 'compare and contrast'

when asked to 'evaluate'

Handling your nerves

Exam nerves are not unusual: it has been concluded that test anxiety arises because of the perception that your performance is being evaluated, that the consequences are likely to be serious and that you are working under the pressure of a time restriction. If you focus on the task at hand, rather than on feeding a downward negative spiral in your thinking patterns, it will help you to keep your nerves under control. In the run-up to your exams, you can practise some simple relaxation techniques that will help you to bring stress under control.

> It is a very good thing if you can interpret your nervous reactions positively—being nervous shows that you care—but the symptoms are more likely to be problematic if you interpret them negatively, pay too much attention to them or allow them to interfere with your exam preparation or performance.

Practices that may help to reduce or buffer the effects of exam stress include:

- listening to music;
- going for a brisk walk;
- simple breathing exercises;
- some muscle relaxation;
- watching a movie;
- having a good laugh;
- doing some exercise;
- relaxing in a bath (with music, if preferred).

The best choice is going to be the one (or combination) of these that works best for you—and this may be discovered by trial and error. Some of the above techniques can be practised on the morning of the exam and even the memory of them can be used just before the exam. For example, you might run over a relaxing tune in your head and have this echo inside you as you enter the exam room. The idea behind all this is that, first, stress levels will be reduced and, second, relaxing thoughts will serve to displace stressful reactions. It has been said that stress is the body's call to take action, but anxiety is a maladaptive response to that call.

Time management

The all-important matter as you approach an exam is to develop the belief that you can take control of the situation. As you work through the list of issues that need to be addressed, you will be able to tick them off one by one. One of the issues about which you will need to be clear before the exam is the length of time that you should allocate to each question. Sometimes, this can be quite simple (although it is always necessary to read the rubric carefully)—for example, if two questions are to be answered in a two-hour paper, you should allow one hour for each question. If it is a two-hour paper with one essay question and five shorter answers, you might allow one hour for the essay and 12 minutes each for the shorter questions—but you must check the weighting for the marks on each question, and you will also need to deduct whatever time it takes you to read over the paper and to choose your questions. More importantly, give yourself some practice on papers similar to those you are likely to face (i.e. past papers).

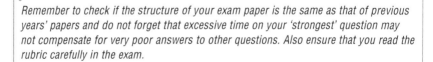

Remember to check if the structure of your exam paper is the same as that of previous years' papers and do not forget that excessive time on your 'strongest' question may not compensate for very poor answers to other questions. Also ensure that you read the rubric carefully in the exam.

Task management

After you have decided on the questions that you wish to address, you need to plan your answers. Some students prefer to plan all outlines and draft work at the beginning, while other prefer to plan and address one answer before proceeding to address the next question.

> *The exam is like conducting an argument, but one in which you have the opportunity to get your views across without interruption.*

Decide on your strategy before you enter the exam room and stick to your plan. When you have completed your draft outline as rough work, you should allocate an appropriate time for each section. This will prevent you from treating of some aspects excessively, while falling short on others. Such careful planning will help you to achieve balance, fluency and symmetry.

> *Remaining aware of time limitations will help you to write succinctly and stay focused on the task, while preventing you from dressing up your responses with unnecessary padding.*

Attend to practical details

This short section is designed to remind you of the practical details that should be attended to in preparation for an exam. There are always students who turn up late, go to the wrong venue, arrive for the wrong exam, or do not turn up at all! Check and recheck that you have all of the details of each exam correctly noted. What you do not need is to arrive late and then have to calm your panic reactions. The exam season is the time when you should aim to be at your best.

Checklist: practical exam details

✓ Check that you have the correct venue and know where it is.
✓ Ensure that the exam time you have noted is accurate.
✓ Allow sufficient time for your journey.
✓ Bring an adequate supply of stationery and a drink.
✓ Fill in required personal details before the exam begins.

The art of 'name dropping'

When studying penology at university, you will be required to cite studies as evidence for your arguments and link these to the names of researchers, scholars or theorists. It will help if you can use the correct dates, or at least the decades. It will also help if you can demonstrate that you have used contemporary sources and have done some independent work. A marker will have dozens, if not hundreds, of scripts to work through and he or she will know if you are just repeating the same phrases from the same sources as everyone else. There is inevitably a certain amount of this that must go on, but there is room for you to add fresh and original touches that demonstrate your independence and sociological imagination.

> Give the clear impression that you have done more than the bare minimum and that you have enthusiasm for the subject.

A politician's answer

Politicians are renowned for refusing to answer questions directly or for evading them through raising other questions. A humorous example is that of a politician being asked: 'Is it true that you always answer questions by asking another?' To this, the politician replied: 'Who told you that?' The point here is that, in an exam, you must make sure that you answer the set question, although there may be other questions that arise out of this that you might want to highlight in your conclusion. As a first principle, you must answer the set question and not try to another that you had hoped to see answer.

EXAMPLE: 'What are the main themes of traditional Marxist approaches to imprisonment?'

Directly relevant points

- Key Marxist thinkers, such as Georg Rusche and Dario Melossi.
- Labour market thesis (the relationship between imprisonment and unemployment).
- Less eligibility, deterrence and the symbolic role of punishment.
- The breaking of links between 'crime' and punishment.
- Historical epochs and functions of punishment.
- Specific criticisms of Marxist penology.

Less relevant points

- Broader themes of Marxist social theory.
- Alternative penalties to imprisonment.
- Philosophical justifications of imprisonment.
- Neo-Marxist and Foucauldian elaborations.
- The development and decline of state welfare.
- Poverty as a social problem.

Although some of the points listed in the second column may be relevant overall, they are not as directly relevant to the given question. Ensure that you focus on the actual question.

Missing your question

Students have often been heard, after an exam, to complain bitterly that the topic they had revised so thoroughly had not been tested in the exam. The first response is, of course, that students should always cover enough topics to avoid selling themselves short in the exam—the habit of 'question spotting' across past papers is always a risky game to play. The reality may be, however, that the question for which the student was looking may have been there, but that the student may simply not have seen it. He or she may have expected the question to be couched in certain words and have not been able to find these when scanning the questions in blind panic. The simple lesson, then, is that you should always read over the exam paper carefully, slowly and thoughtfully— and that this is a practice that will be time well spent.

Write it down

If you write down the question that you have chosen to address and, perhaps, quietly mouth it to yourself, you are more likely to process fully its true meaning and intent. Think of how easy it is to misunderstand a question that has been put to you verbally, because you have misinterpreted the tone or emphasis.

Pursue a critical approach

In degree courses, you are usually expected to write critically rather than merely descriptively, although it may be necessary to use some minimal descriptive substance as the raw material for your debate. Given that most questions require some form of critical evaluation of the evidence, you will need to address issues one by one from different standpoints. What you should *not* do, however, is digress into a tangent about irrelevant and abstract information.

Analyse the parts

A good essay cannot be constructed without reference to its parts. Furthermore, the parts will arise as you break the question down into the components that it suggests to you. Although the breaking down of a question into components is not sufficient for an excellent essay, it is a necessary starting point.

EXAMPLE 1: 'Evaluate the advantages and disadvantages of promoting concrete alternatives to prison'

This is a straightforward question in that you have two major sections: advantages and disadvantages. You are left with the choice of the issues that you wish to address and you can arrange these in the order you prefer. Your aim should be to ensure that you do not have a lopsided view of this, even if you feel quite strongly one way or the other.

EXAMPLE 2: 'Trace, in a critical manner, Western society's changing attitudes to the corporal punishment of children'

In this case, you might want to consider the role of governments, the church, schools, parents and the media. You will, however, need to provide some reference points to the past, because you are being asked to address the issue of change. There will also be scope to look at where the strongest influences for change arise and where the strongest resistance comes from. You might argue that the changes have been either dramatic or evolutionary.

When asked to 'discuss'

Students often ask how much of their own opinion they should include in an essay. In a 'discussion', when you raise one issue, another one might arise out of it. Many tutors have introduced their lectures by saying that they are going to 'unpack' the arguments. When you unpack an object (such as a new desk that has to be assembled), you first remove the overall packaging, such as a large box, and then proceed to remove the covers from all the component parts. After that, you attempt to assemble all of the parts, according to the given design, so that they hold together in the intended manner. In a discussion, your aim should be not only to identify and define all of the parts that contribute, but also to show where they fit (or do not fit) into the overall picture.

Checklist: features of a response to a 'discuss' question

✓ It contains a chain of issues that lead into each other in sequence.
✓ It has clear shape and direction, which is unfolded in the progression of the argument.
✓ It is underpinned by reference to findings and certainties.
✓ It identifies those issues for which doubt remains.

If a 'critique' is requested

One example that might help to clarify what is involved in a 'critique' is the hotly debated topic of the physical punishment of children. It would be important, in the interest of balance and fairness, to present all sides and shades of the argument. You would then look at whether there is available evidence to support each argument, and you might introduce issues that have been coloured by prejudice, tradition, religion and legislation. You would aim to identify those arguments that are based on emotion and intuition, and to get down to those arguments that really have solid evidence-based support. Finally, you would need to flag up where the strongest evidence appears to lie and also to identify issues that appear to be inconclusive. It would be expected that you should, if possible, arrive at some certainties.

If asked to 'compare and contrast'

When asked to 'compare and contrast', you should be thinking in terms of similarities and differences. You should ask what the two issues share in common and what features of each are distinct.

EXAMPLE: 'Compare and contrast penal reductionist and abolitionist approaches to the penal system'

Similarities

- Both promote humanitarian changes to dealing with offenders.
- Both highlight the pains of imprisonment and penal controversies, such as the punishment of the mentally ill, self-inflicted deaths and racism in prison.
- Both promote the human rights of offenders.
- Both highlight the necessity of democratic and legally accountable means of dealing with offenders.
- Both call for alternatives to prison.

Contrasts

- The legitimacy of punishment and the punitive rationale are conceived differently in each approach.
- Reductionists focus mainly on changing the criminal justice system, whereas abolitionists highlight socio-economic and political contexts.
- There are differences in the proposed content of human rights.
- Reductionists believe that prisons can be reformed, whereas abolitionists point to the inherent brutalities of imprisonment.
- Abolitionists call for radical alternatives, while reductionists look to probation and more mainstream community penalties.

When asked to 'evaluate'

When thinking about how to approach a question that asks you to 'evaluate' a theory or concept in penology, you should consider:

- Has the theory stood the test of time?
- Is there a supportive evidence base that is not easily overturned?
- Are there questionable elements that should be challenged?
- Does more recent evidence point to a need for modification?
- Is the theory robust and likely to be around for the foreseeable future?
- Might it be strengthened through being merged with other theories?

It should be noted that the words presented in the above examples might not always be the exact words that will appear on your exam script—you might, for example, find 'analyse', 'outline', or 'investigate', etc.—but the best advice is to check over past exam papers and to familiarise yourself with the words that are most recurrent.

part four

additional resources

Core areas: **glossary**
bibliography

glossary

Abolitionism	A theoretical and political perspective holding that the penal system creates, rather than provides solutions to, **social problems**. Abolitionists call for new understandings of the social harms that we face and for **radical alternatives** to current ways of responding to **wrongdoing**.
Actuarialism	An insurance technique that can be deployed to manage **'crime'** by analysing the distribution of **risk** within aggregate populations.
Administrative penology	A way of theorising and analysing punishments intimately associated with, and often funded by, the government.
Authoritarian populism	An explanation of how punitive and repressive laws can gain widespread consent among the public.
Bifurcation	The attempt to reserve imprisonment for serious and dangerous offenders, while at the same time giving low-risk offenders **community penalties**.
Bloody Code	How capital punishments were deployed in eighteenth-century England as a means of exercising ideological control.
Carceral society	The argument made by Michel Foucault (French philosopher) that changes in

the penal system in the nineteenth century were not inspired by humanitarian benevolence, but rather by the deepening and expansion of disciplinary **power**.

Causation

The assertion that one event or set of circumstances inevitably cause(s) another event or set of circumstances to occur.

Civilisation

The advancement of society to a higher level of **moral**, cultural and social values. Emile Durkheim and penologists following in the tradition of Norbert Elias have applied the civilisation process to forms of **punishment**.

Community penalties

Non-custodial penal sanctions.

Comparative analysis

The selection and study of two or more cases to highlight similarities and differences. This can involve comparing penal systems and forms of **punishment** in different countries.

Contestability

The opening up of the provision of **rehabilitation** for offenders to contest from both the public and private sectors.

Correlation

When two or more phenomena occur at the same time, but are not necessarily linked.

'Crime'

The term applied to refer to certain social harms, illegalities and forms of **wrongdoing**. A 'crime' is a **social construction** that is shaped by specific legal, historical and spatial contexts. The constitution of what a 'crime' entails is essentially contested, and depends on the theoretical and political position of the definer.

Criminalisation	The application of the 'criminal' label.
Criminal justice system	The collective name given to state agencies that respond to illegal behaviours. These include the police, the courts, and **probation** and prison services.
Crisis	A term indicating that, if action is not taken soon to address current problems and difficulties, a breakdown or disaster will occur.
Culture	The norms and values of a given society or institution.
Dangerousness	A social and historical construction that has referred to a number of different groups of offenders. Today, it generally refers to violent, sexual and persistent property offenders.
Dark figure	The very large amount of **'crime'** and harm in society that is not covered in official statistics.
Decarceration	Moving away from imprisonment as the central penal sanction.
Decency	A humanitarian ethos to prison work introduced by former Director General Martin Narey. This is a vague concept that implies treating prisoners as fellow human beings, developing relationships with prisoners, ensuring that prisoners receive their lawful entitlements, and a commitment to reducing racism, self-inflicted deaths and prison officer brutality.
Dehumanisation	A process under which the basic prerequisites of human life are undermined and deliberately removed, resulting in alienation and profound human suffering.

Democracy	The unhindered participation of all people in processes of shared decision making. In a democracy, all human voices are deemed valid and of equal worth in the creation of social norms.
Denunciation	When a **'crime'**, social harm, or wrong is symbolically denounced, often through **punishment**.
Deterrence	The philosophical justification of **punishment** that looks to deter individuals or wider members of society from future lawbreaking through efficient and effective penal sanctions.
Deviance	Social behaviour that deviates from the dominant cultural norms and values.
Enlightenment	The philosophical movement maintaining that man and woman can use human reason and rational thought to explain social phenomena.
False negatives	Linked to the philosophical justification of **incapacitation**. This arises when an **offender** is predicted not to reoffend, but does so.
False positives	When an **offender** is predicted to reoffend, but does not do so. This is difficult to assess because the offender has been incapacitated.
Feminism	A sociological, philosophical and political tradition that calls for the fair and equitable treatment of women. There are a number of feminist perspectives, including liberal feminism, Marxist feminism, radical feminism, Black feminism, postmodern feminism and socialist feminism.

Functionalism	When a given social institution, such as prison, is defined as meeting certain prerequisite needs for society to successfully function. This 'functional fit' does not necessarily have to correspond with the official aims of the given institution. Marxist and Foucauldian theories are sometimes referred to as 'left functionalism', because they highlight the way in which prisons function in the interests of the powerful.
Globalisation	The increasing homogeneity of global economies, and its implications for national politics and **culture**.
Governmentality	A highly influential theoretical perspective derived from the later works of Michel Foucault. Governmentality theorists focus on governing technologies and mentalities that privilege **risk** and security. The major drawback is that this perspective is largely descriptive.
Governmental sovereignty	The political criteria that defines the legitimate goals and role of the government.
Harm reduction policies	These are policies that prioritise the safety of those who engage in risky and potentially harmful practices. The overall goal is reducing harm—such as the spread of HIV through infected needles—than reducing the prevalence of a given activity.
Hegemony	The dominant idea or means of interpretation. It implies intellectual and **moral** leadership, and is crucial in the creation of consent.
Humane containment	An aim of imprisonment that claims that, although prisons cannot be

justified through **rehabilitation**, prisons should treat those they contain as humanely as possible.

Human rights

A concept that is based on the recognition of the innate dignity of a fellow human beings. Human rights provide a politically acceptable **moral** framework through which we can critique the infamies of the present, acknowledge human suffering and promote tolerance of diversity. They also have a latent function in promoting the positive obligations and legal duties of the powerful to protect the rights of citizens.

Human Rights Act (HRA)

The Human Rights Act 1998, which came into force on the 2 October 2000.

Ideology

A set of beliefs, values and ideas that shape the way in which people understand the world. For neo-Marxists, ideology is important in winning the battle for hearts and minds on how we should respond to wrongdoers.

Incapacitation

A philosophical justification of **punishment** that calls for the removal of the **offender's** physical capacity to offend. This can be done through the death penalty, banishment or **incarceration**.

Incarceration

The process of placing people into institutions such as the prison.

Just deserts

A justification of sentencing that is tied to the philosophical justification of **retribution**. In short: you get the **punishment** you deserve by receiving a sentence that is proportionate to the offence you have committed.

Key performance indicators/targets	The targets that the prison service sets each financial year.
Labelling theory	A sociological theory that examines the social consequences of applying negative labels to individuals and groups. Rooted in the symbolic interactionism of George Herbert Mead, penologists have focused on the stigma and **dehumanisation** that is created through the 'prisoner' label.
Labour market	A term used to describe the relations between the buyers (capitalists) and sellers (workers) of labour **power**. Penologists have been particularly interested in the division of labour (Durkheim) and the consequences of unemployment for the form that **punishment** takes in a given society (Rusche).
Late modernity	A term used to describe changes in the **labour market**, families, communications, **mass media** and **culture** in Western societies since the 1970s.
Law and order society	The famous argument made by sociologist Stuart Hall that concerns about '**crime**' and lawbreaking have become central to current forms of political debate.
Legitimacy	The **moral** and political validity of a given state of affairs. This is a contested concept, with some penologists arguing legitimacy is dependent on: (1) whether people *believe* something is legitimate; (2) whether a set of circumstances adheres to *people's beliefs*; or (3) whether validity should be based on *normative criteria*, such as meeting the requirements of **social justice** and **human rights** standards.

Less eligibility	A doctrine under which the conditions of imprisonment must not be higher than the living conditions of the poorest labourer. This perspective is tied to the philosophical justification of **deterrence**.
Managerialism	Highly influential credos that claimed that changes in the management of the criminal justice would lead to improved performance and lower costs.
Marxism	Sociological, political and philosophical perspective, rooted in the work of Karl Marx, that argues against the logic of capitalism, calling instead for forms of **political economy** and **governmental sovereignty** that are rooted in meeting human needs.
Mass media	Institutions of communication that broadcast, or distribute, information. The media include newspapers, magazines, the Internet, television, radio and the cinema.
Methodology	The techniques deployed to undertake empirical studies to glean knowledge of social practices. Research methodology can include observation, interviews and questionnaires.
Ministry of Justice	A government department established in May 2007 to head the correctional services (prisons and **probation**) in England and Wales.
Modernity	A period of time since the eighteenth century that is closely associated with the rise of industrial society, liberal democratic governance and the intellectual drives of the **enlightenment**.

Moral	Refers to the 'right thing to do' in a given set of circumstances.
Moral panic	A term introduced by Stan Cohen in the 1970s to explain how society sometimes overreacts to a person, or group of people, who have challenged societal norms, and calls for a disproportionate increase in **social control** and repression.
Neo-abolitionism	A modernist and humanist perspective that integrates the insights of symbolic interactionism with the political analysis of criminologies that are inspired by neo-Marxism and the **moral** framework of penal **abolitionism**.
Neoliberalism	A term that describes a set of ideologies that privilege the free market. Neoliberalism promotes minimal state intervention for the provision of social welfare, but argues that we should retain a strong authoritarian state.
NOMS	National Offender Management Service.
Normalisation	This term has been applied in two very different ways in **penology**. Roy King and Rod Morgan used this term in the 1980s to argue that prison life should be as *normal* as possible in relation to that on the outside. This use of the term is closely linked to debates on prison conditions. The French philosopher Michel Foucault, however, used the term 'normalisation' to highlight how penalties have been used in an attempt to make offenders normal. This use of the term is closely associated with the ideas of **bifurcation** and **rehabilitation**.

OASys	Offender assessment system—used by **probation** officers to assess **risk**.
Offender	The term used to describe a person who has breached societal rules or laws.
Offender pathways	Current government initiative around **resettlement** that aims to identify the criminogenic and social needs of offenders, and to provide policies that can address each one of these factors.
Pains of imprisonment	A term used to describe the inherent deprivations of prison life. Gresham Sykes (1958) described the *'pains of imprisonment'* for male prisoners as the deprivation of liberty, heterosexual sex, goods and services, autonomy and security. Women prisoners are likely to experience other pains in addition to these.
Panopticon	A design prison by Jeremy Bentham that aimed to maximise prisoner surveillance as a means of instilling discipline.
Parole	A word derived from the French term *parole d'homneur,* meaning to give your word of honour. Parole was first introduced in the English penal system through the 'ticket of leave system' in the nineteenth century.
Penal accountability	The principle that responses to wrongdoers should be premised upon the rule of law, legal guarantees and procedural safeguards rooted in the principles of fairness, transparency and equality. Legal accountability places ethical boundaries and preclusions on the extent of state interventions.

Penal controversy	This is a strongly disputed and contentious form of penal practice that leads to questions about its **moral** and/or political **legitimacy**.
Penal expansionism	Referring to an approach based on increasing prison numbers and prison capacity. This approach currently shapes **penal policy** in England and Wales.
Penalisation	The application of the penal sanction.
Penality	The study of the ideas, principles, policies and practices of the penal system, alongside their broader socio-economic, historical, intellectual and political contexts. Penality looks to understand **punishment** and regulation, both within and beyond state institutions.
Penal performance	The measurements used to assess if a prison is meeting the standards set by the prison service. This can be linked to managerial targets or based on *Measurement of the Quality of Prison Life* surveys, which aim to assess the **moral** performance of imprisonment.
Penal policy	A collective term for government and **criminal justice system** documents detailing the main aims, principles and ideas that shape the practices of penal institutions.
Penal reductionism	Calls for a massive reduction in prisoner numbers and the penal estate. Penal reductionists often argue that the capacity for imprisonment should be at no higher than 20,000 places.
Penitentiary	A term used to describe the first convict prisons of the UK in the nineteenth

century. Drawing upon the meanings of the Christian term 'penitence', the penitentiary was intended to be an institution that would lead those incarcerated to repent of their **wrongdoing**.

Penology
The sociological and philosophical study of penal institutions. In recent times, in the UK, its primary focus has been on evaluating the practices and **legitimacy** of imprisonment.

Persistency
A term largely applied today to prolific property offending by working-class boys.

Persistency principle
A belief that offenders should be punished not only based on their current offence, but also on past offending. This approach has gained increasing influence with the changes to sentencing following the Halliday Report (2001) and the Criminal Justice Act 2003.

Political economy
The manner in which the economy is organised in a given society.

Political theory
The study of the organisation and exercise of power, including that of the state and government.

Positivism
The belief that scientific knowledge and methods can be used in the social sciences to study humans. Positivism has significant implications for research ethics and **methodology**. Although it has been intellectually discredited in the academy, positivistic studies still have political and policy influence.

Postmodernism
A theoretical perspective and 'state of mind' that is rooted in the belief that we

have seen an end to metanarratives (big stories) and a loss of confidence in social progress. Without absolute values, we can no longer have certainty in knowledge or uncover the truth.

Poverty

Refers to the inability to meet necessary needs and to live a full human life.

Power

A term that refers to an ability to make somebody do something that they would not normally do.

Power/knowledge

A term introduced by Michel Foucault to describe the manner in which people in positions of **power** have the ability to present certain realities as the truth.

Pressure group

This is an organisation that looks to: lobby parliament for changes in the law; inform the general public on a particular matter; and/or provide specialist support to members of the public who have been affected by a particular problem, such as the families of those who die in custody. A pressure group will reflect certain political beliefs and values.

Prison disturbances

The term sometimes used to describe prisoner rebellion, revolts and riots. Used most famously by Lord Woolf in 1991.

Prisoner populations

This can be measured by various means: the average daily population; the rate per 100,000 of the overall population; examining the numbers who are sentenced to prison each year. These are not objective data, but are produced for the needs of the penal system itself.

Prison works

The argument popularised by Michael Howard and Charles Murray that, if used ruthlessly enough, prison might act as a means of **deterrence** and **incapacitation**.

Probation

A state institution that was set up to befriend offenders, but which, in recent times, has become focused on **risk assessment**.

Punishment

The deliberate infliction of pain.

Punitiveness

The extent to which **punishment** and the punitive rationale is embedded within an individual or **culture**.

Radical alternatives

The argument made by penal abolitionists that we need to rethink how we respond to **social problems**. Radical alternatives include promoting forms of redress, social policies that are rooted in the principle of **social justice** and which look to address structural inequities, and positive community interventions that give young people (the staple diet of the **criminal justice system**) constructive things to do with their time.

Rational choice theory

Intimately tied with the philosophical justification of **deterrence**, this perspective is predicated on the assumption that human beings make rational decisions before they break the law. Severity and certainty of sentence are supposed to impact upon this decision-making process

Recidivism rates

The level of reoffending

Reform

(1) A philosophical justification of **punishment**, which claims that punishment—and specifically imprisonment—can be used to change the prisoner into a better person. Today, this meaning of reform is used interchangeably with

rehabilitation. (2) Reform is now often used to refer to changes made to penal regimes and attempts to make prisons more humane environments.

Rehabilitation

A philosophical justification of **punishment**, which claims that punishments can be used to restore an **offender** to his or her previous competency. Although tied to a medical model, the term is used in the broader sense as a means of helping offenders to desist from **crime**.

Relative surplus population

A group of people who are unemployed, but who can join the workforce in times of economic growth. The term is largely used by Marxist penologists.

Remand

The term used to refer to the time during which a person is held in prison awaiting trial. Remand prisoners are often held in worse conditions than those of convicted prisoners.

Resettlement

The current policy aiming to help prisoners to reintegrate back into the community on release from prison.

Responsibilisation strategies

An argument that, under neoliberal forms of governance, the powerless are given responsibilities rather than rights. Responsibilities are removed from the state for providing security and safety for the general public.

Restorative justice

A way of responding to crimes, problems and harms that is rooted in the principles of mediation and reparation. Since the Crime and Disorder Act 1998, restorative justice has become an important part of government policy.

Retribution	The philosophical justification of **punishment**, which claims that people deserve to be punished for their past crimes. Rooted in the principles of 'two wrongs make a right', the philosophy explains why we need to respond to **wrongdoing**, but does not explain why that must entail the deliberate infliction of pain.
Risk	A means of calculating danger, harm, injury, damage or loss. This is now the dominant way of conceiving **social problems**.
Risk assessment	Assessment of an **offender**'s likelihood to perform future criminal activity.
Risk society	An influential argument made by German sociologist Ulrich Beck that society is now more characterised by the distribution of ills than it is by the distribution of goods.
Scapegoating	A term that refers to the practice of wrongly blaming somebody for a **crime** or harm. People from minority ethnic groups and poor backgrounds are most likely to be scapegoated.
'Security, control and justice'	An approach to **penal policy**, as advocated by Lord Justice Woolf in 1991.
Social construction	The manner in which meanings are defined, judged and applied to social life. Understandings of social phenomena are shaped by time, place, **culture** and historical contexts.
Social control	A very broad term, which relates to the mechanisms that are deployed to ensure

that people conform to social expectations. This includes informal social controls, such as the family and schooling, and formal social controls, such as the police and prisons.

Social exclusion

Often used in place of the term '**poverty**', social exclusion refers to many ways in which people can be barred from participating in society's social, economic, political and cultural systems.

Social harm perspective

A radical argument that moves beyond those harms defined by the criminal law to take seriously all harms that impact upon people, from cradle to grave.

Social justice

This principle requires the equitable redistribution of the social product, allowing individuals to meet their necessary needs. Alongside this, it requires a rebalancing of **power**, the reducing of vulnerabilities, and the fostering of trust, security and social inclusion. This principle supposes that all wrongdoers and social harms are dealt with fairly and appropriately. It also implies recognition and respect for the shared humanity of offenders.

Social problems

Refers to issues that are understood as problematic within their social and historical context. What is included in the definition of social problems depends, at any given time, on the influence of those who have the **power** to define.

Socio-economic context

The social and economic circumstances surrounding a person's lived realities.

Sociology

An academic discipline that studies society. Sociological theories inform a number of penological studies and the 'sociology of **deviance**'.

Sub-proletariat

A term used by Marxist penologists in place of the term 'underclass', which implies a permanent class that exists below the proletariat. The sub-proletariat consists of economically marginalised and socially excluded people at the bottom of the social hierarchy. They are often members of the **relative surplus population** (unemployment) and are the people most likely to end up in our prisons.

Transcarceration

When people are moved from one institution, such as the mental asylum, to another, such as the prison.

Treatment and training ideology

The term used to describe the dominant rationale of the prison service in England and Wales from the 1920s until the 1970s.

Utilitarianism

The philosophy that social policies should be based on the principle of the greatest happiness of the greatest number of people. It has been challenged, because it raises considerable problems for the **human rights** of minority groups.

Victim

The term used in the **criminal justice system** to describe the person who has been harmed through a criminal act. The word 'victim', however, has been challenged and many feminists have argued that the term 'survivor' is a more accurate description.

Welfare through punishment

The argument that social welfare is now provided to the poor and vulnerable only after they have been caught up within the penal web.

What works

An approach to **rehabilitation** that is rooted in the principles of cognitive behaviouralism. The 'what works' agenda dominates current accredited programmes in prisons in England and Wales.

Woman-wise penology

A feminist approach that is championed by Pat Carlen, who argues that responses to women who offend should be rooted in principles of empowerment.

Wrongdoing

A **moral** term used to describe inappropriate, harmful and potentially illegal behaviour.

bibliography

Advisory Council on Misuse of Drugs (1996) *Part III: Drug Misusers and the Prison System—An Integrated Approach*, London: HMSO.

Barak-Glantz, I (1981) 'Toward a conceptual schema of prison management styles', *The Prison Journal*, 61(2), pp. 42–60.

Barton, A, Corteen, K, Scott, DG and Whyte, D (eds) (2006) *Expanding the Criminological Imagination*, Cullompton: Willan Publishing.

Bauman, Z (1989) *Modernity and the Holocaust*, Cambridge: Polity Press.

Bean, P (1981) *Punishment: A Philosophical and Criminological Inquiry*, Oxford: Martin Robertson.

Beccaria, CB (1764; 1986) *Essays on Crimes and Punishment*, Indianapolis, IN: Hackett Publishing Ltd.

Blair, A (2004) 'Foreword: Prime Minister' in HM Government, *Cutting Crime, Delivering Justice: A Strategic Plan for Criminal Justice 2004–8*, London: HMSO, pp. 5–6.

Bottoms, A (1977) 'Reflections on the renaissance of dangerousness', *Howard Journal*, 16(2), pp. 70–97.

Bottoms, A (1990) 'The aims of imprisonment', in D Garland (ed) *Justice, Guilt and Forgiveness in the Penal System*, Edinburgh: University of Edinburgh.

Bottoms, A, Rex, S and Robinson, G (eds) (2004) *Alternatives to Prison: Options for an Insecure Society*, Cullompton: Willan Publishing.

Bowker, L (1977) *Prisoner Subcultures*, Lexington, MA: DC Heath and Co.

Bowling, B and Phillips, C (2002) *Racism, Crime and Justice*, London: Longman.

Box, S (1987) *Recession, Crime and Punishment*, London: Macmillan.

Box, S and Hale, C (1982) 'Economic crises and the rising prisoner population', *Crime and Social Justice*, 17, pp. 20–35.

Boyle, J (1977) *A Sense Of Freedom*, London: Pan Books.

Braithwaite, J and Pettit, P (1990) *Not Just Deserts: A Republican Theory of Criminal Justice*, Oxford: Clarendon Press.

Brownlee, I (1998) *Community Punishment: A Critical Introduction*, London: Longman.

Bryans, S and Jones, R (eds) (2001) *Prisons and the Prisoner*, London: HMSO.

Carlen, P (1983) *Women's Imprisonment*, London: Routledge.

Carlen, P and Worrall, A (2004) *Analysing Women's Imprisonment*, Cullompton: Willan Publishing.

Carter, P (2004) *Managing Offenders, Reducing Crime: A New Approach*, London: Home Office (the 'Carter Review').

Carrabine, E (2004) *Power, Discourse and Resistance: A Genealogy of the Strangeways Prison Riot*, Aldershot: Ashgate Publishing.

Cavadino, M and Dignan, J (2006) *Penal Systems: A Comparative Approach*, London: Sage.

Cavadino, M and Dignan, J (2007) *The Penal System*, 4th edn, London: Sage.

Chigwada-Bailey, R (2003) *Black Women's Experience of Criminal Justice*, Winchester: Waterside Press.

Christie, N (2000) *Crime Control as Industry: Towards Gulags, Western Style*, 2nd edn London: Routledge.

Clarke, J and Newman, J (1997) *The Managerial State*, London: Sage.

Clemmer, D (1948) *The Prison Community*, New York: Holt, Reinhart and Winston.

Codd, H (2008) *In the Shadow of the Prison*, Cullompton: Willan Publishing.

Cohen, S (1985) *Visions of Social Control: Crime Punishment and Classification*, Cambridge: Polity Press.

Cohen, S (2001) *States of Denial: Knowing About Atrocities and Suffering*, Cambridge: Polity Press.

Cohen, S and Scull, A (eds) (1983) *Social Control and the State*, Oxford: Blackwell.

Cohen, S and Taylor, L (1972; 1981) *Psychological Survival: The Experience Of Long-Term Imprisonment*, 2nd edn, Harmondsworth: Penguin.

Cohen, S and Taylor, L (1978) *Prison Secrets*, London: RAP/NCCL.

Coyle, A (2005) *Understanding Prisons*, Milton Keynes: Open University Press.

Crawley, E (2004) *Doing Prison Work: The Public and Private Lives of Prison Officers*, Cullompton: Willan Publishing.

Creighton, S, King, V and Arnott, H (2005) *Prisoners and the Law*, 3rd edn, Haywards Heath: Tottel Publishing.

Cressey, R (1959) *The Prison*, New York: Anchor Press.

De Haan, W (1990) *The Politics of Redress*, London: Sage.

DiIulio, JJ (1990) *Governing Prisons: A Comparative Study of Correctional Management*, London: Free Press.

Dostoevsky, F (1860) *House of the Dead*, Harmondsworth: Penguin.

Durkheim, E (1893; 1984) *Division of Labour*, London: Macmillan.

Durkheim, E (1912; 2001) *The Elementary Forms of Religious Life*, Oxford: Oxford University Press.

Elias, N (1939; 1984) *The Civilising Process*, two vols, Oxford: Blackwell.

Emery, FE (1970) *Freedom and Justice Within Walls: The Bristol Prison Experiment*, London: Tavistock.

Emsley, C (1996) *Crime and Society in England 1750–1900*, London: Longman.

Feeley, M and Simon, J (1994) 'Actuarial justice: the emerging new criminal law', in D Nelken (ed) *The Futures Of Criminology*, London: Sage, pp. 173–201.

Fitzgerald, M and Sim, J (1982) *British Prisons*, 2nd edn, Oxford: Blackwell.

Flew, A (1954) 'The justification of punishment', in HB Acton (ed) (1969) *The Philosophy of Punishment*, London: Macmillan, pp. 83–101.

Flynn, N (1998) *Introduction to Prisons and Imprisonment*, Winchester: Waterside Press.

Foucault, M (1977) *Discipline and Punish: The Birth of the Prison*, Harmondsworth: Penguin.

Gamble, A (1988) *The Free Market and the Strong State*, London: Macmillan.

Garland, D (1990) *Punishment and Modern Society: A Study in Social Theory*, Oxford: Oxford University Press.

Garland, D and Young, P (eds) (1983) *The Power to Punish: Contemporary Penality and Social Analysis*, Oxford: Heinemann Education Books Ltd.

Gattrell, VAC (1994) *The Hanging Tree*, Oxford: Oxford University Press.

Gelsthorpe, L and Morgan, R (eds) (2007) *Handbook of Probation*, Cullompton: Willan Publishing.

Goffman, E (1956) *The Presentation of the Self in Everyday Life*, Edinburgh: University of Edinburgh.

Goffman, E (1963) *Asylums: Essays on the Situation of Mental Patients and Other Inmates*, Harmondsworth: Penguin.

Golash, D (2005) *The Case Against Punishment*, New York: New York University Press.

Green, S, Johnson, H and Young, P (2008) *Understanding Crime Data*, Milton Keynes: Open University Press.

Hall, S, Critcher, C, Jefferson, T, Clark, J and Roberts, B (1978) *Policing the Crisis: Mugging the State and Law and Order*, London: Macmillan.

Halliday, J (2001) *Making Punishment Work: Report of a Review of the Sentencing Framework for England and Wales*, London: Home Office Communication Directorate (the 'Halliday Report').

Hannah-Moffat, K (2001) *Punishment in Disguise: Penal Governance and Federal Imprisonment of Women in Canada*, Toronto: University of Toronto Press.

Harding, R (1997) *Private Prisons and Public Accountability*, Milton Keynes: Open University Press.

Hay, D (1975) 'Property, authority and the criminal law' in D Hay, P Linebaugh, JG Rule, EP Thompson and C Winslow (eds) *Albion's Fatal Tree*, Harmondsworth: Penguin, pp. 17–64.

Heidensohn, F (1985) *Women and Crime*, London: Macmillan.

Hernstein, R and Murray, C (1994) *The Bell Curve: Intelligence and Class Structure in American Life*, New York: Free Press.

HM Chief Inspector of Prisons (1998) *Annual Report 1997–8 of HM Chief Inspector of Prisons*, London: HMSO.

HM Chief Inspector of Prisons (1999) *Suicide is Everyone's Concern: A Thematic Review*, London: HMSO.

HM Chief Inspector of Prisons (2005) *Parallel Lives*, London: HMSO.

HM Prison Service (1993) *HM Prison Service Corporate Plan 1993–6*, London: HMSO.

HM Prison Service (1998a) *Prison Service Strategic Framework*, London: HMSO.

HM Prison Service (1998b) *Tackling Drugs in Prison: The Prison Service Drug Strategy*, London: HMSO.

HM Prison Service (2000) *The Human Rights Act: What Does It Mean for the Service?*, London: HM Prison Service.

HM Prison Service (2003a) *Annual Report and Accounts Apr 2002–Mar 2003*, London: HMSO.

HM Prison Service (2003b) *Prison Service Action Plan*, London: HM Prison Service.

HM Prison Service (2003c) *Re-Introduction of Disinfecting Tablets*, Prison Service Instruction (PSI) 53/2003, London: HM Prison Service.

HM Prison Service (2004) *Management of Segregation Units and Management of Prisoners Under Rule 45 (YOI Rule 49)*, Revised Prison Service Order (PSO) 1700, London: HM Prison Service.

HM Prison Service (2005) *Annual Report and Accounts Apr 2004–Mar 2005*, London: HMSO.

Hobhouse, S and Brockway, AF (1922) *English Prisons Today*, London: Longmans, Green and Co.

Home Office (1979) *Report of the Committee of Inquiry into the United Kingdom Prison Service*, London: HMSO (the 'May Report').

Home Office (1990) *Crime, Justice and Protecting the Public*, London: HMSO.

Home Office (1996) *Protecting the Public: The Government's Strategy on Crime in England and Wales*, London: HMSO.

Home Office (2002) *Justice for All*, London: HMSO.

Home Office (2003) *Recidivism Rates 2001–2*, London: HMSO.

Home Office (2004a) *Reducing Crime, Changing Lives: The Government's Plans for Transforming the Management of Offenders*, London: HMSO.

Home Office (2004b) *Reducing Reoffending: National Action Plan*, London: HMSO.

Home Office (2004c) *Cutting Crime, Delivering Justice: A Strategic Plan For Criminal Justice 2004–8*, London: HMSO.

Home Office (2006) *Respect Action Plan*, London: HMSO.

Honderich, T (2006) *Punishment: The Supposed Justifications Revisited*, London: Pluto Press.

Hudson, B (1993) *Penal Policy and Social Justice*, London: Macmillan.

Hudson B (2003) *Understanding Justice*, 2nd edn, Milton Keynes: Open University Press.

Hunt, A and Wickham, G (1994) *Foucault and the Law*, London: Pluto Press.

Ignatieff, M (1978) *A Just Measure of Pain*, Harmondsworth: Penguin.

INQUEST (2006) 'Statistics on self-inflicted deaths', available online at www.inquest.org.uk (accessed 30 May 2006).

INQUEST (2007a) 'Briefing: the death of Sarah Campbell', available online at www.inquest.org.uk (accessed 20 May 2007).

INQUEST (2007b) 'Statistics on self-inflicted deaths', available online at www.inquest.org.uk (accessed 21 September 2007).

Irwin, J (1970) *The Felon*, Englewood Cliffs, NJ: Prentice Hall.

Jacobs, JB (1978) *Stateville: The Penitentiary in Mass Society*, Chicago, IL: University of Chicago.

Jewkes, Y (2002) *Captive Audience: Media, Masculinity and Power in Prisons*, Cullompton: Willan Publishing.

Jewkes, Y (ed) (2007a) *Handbook of Prisons*, Cullompton: Willan Publishing.

Jewkes, Y (2007b) *Media and Crime*, 2nd edn, London: Sage.

Jewkes, Y and Bennett, J (2007) *Dictionary of Prisons and Punishment*, Cullompton: Willan Publishing.

Jewkes, Y and Johnson, H (eds) (2006) *Prison Readings: A Critical Introduction to Prisons and Imprisonment*, Cullompton: Willan Publishing.

Jones, H and Cornes, P (1973) *Open Prisons*, London: Routledge.

Kauffman, K (1988) *Prison Officers and Their World*, Cambridge, MA: Harvard University Press.

Keene, J (1997) 'Drug misuse in prison', *Journal of the Howard League*, 36(1), pp. 28–41.

Keith, B (2006) *The Zahid Mubarek Inquiry, Vols 1 and 2*, London: HMSO (the 'Keith Report').

King, R and Elliott, K (1977) *Albany*, London: Routledge Kegan Paul.

King, RD and Morgan, R (1980) *The Future of the Prison System*, Farnborough: Gower Publishing.

Learmont, J, (1995) *Review of Prison Service Security in England and Wales and the Escapes from Parkhurst Prison on Tuesday 3 January 1995*, London: HMSO (the 'Learmont Report').

Leech, M (1992) *A Product of the System*, London: Victor Gollancz.

Liebling, A (2004) *Prisons and their Moral Performance: A Study of Values, Quality and Prison Life*, Oxford: Oxford University Press.

Liebling, A and Price, D (2001; 2007) *The Prison Officer*, Cullompton: Willan Publishing.

Livingstone, S, Owen, T and MacDonald, A (2003) *Prison Law*, 3rd edn, Oxford: Oxford University Press.

Lombardo, LX (1981) *Guards Imprisoned: Correctional Officers at Work*, New York: Elsevier

Maguire, M, Vagg, J and Morgan, R (eds) (1985) *Accountability and Prisons: Opening Up a Closed World*, London: Tavistock.

Mathiesen, T (1965) *Defences of the Weak: Sociological Study of a Norwegian Correctional Institution*, London: Tavistock.

Mathiesen, T (1974) *The Politics of Abolition*, Oxford: Martin Robertson.

Mathiesen, T (2006) *Prison On Trial*, 3rd edn, Winchester: Waterside.

Matthews, R (1999) *Doing Time*, London: Palgrave.

McConville, S (1995) 'The Victorian Prison: England, 1865–1965', in N Morris and DJ Rothman (eds) *The Oxford History of the Prison*, Oxford: Oxford University Press, pp. 117–50.

Melossi, D (ed) (1999) *The Sociology of Punishment*, Aldershot: Ashgate

Mills, CW (1959) *The Sociological Imagination*, New York: Oxford University Press.

Morris, N and Rothman, D (1998) *The Oxford History of the Prison*, Oxford: Oxford University Press.

Morris, TP and Morris, P (1963) *Pentonville: A Sociological Study of an English Prison*, London: Routledge Kegan Paul.

Mountbatten, Earl (1966) *Report of the Inquiry into Prison Escapes and Security Command 3175*, London: HMSO (the 'Mountbatten Report').

Murray, C (1984) *Losing Ground: American Social Policy, 1950–80*, New York: Basic Books.

Murray, C (1997) *Does Prison Work?*, London: IEA.

Newburn, T (2007) *Criminology*, Cullompton: Willan Publishing.

Northern Ireland Prison Service (2006) *Annual Report*, Belfast: NIPS.

Parenti, C (1999) *Lockdown America: Police and Prisons in the Age of Crisis*, New York: Verso Press.

Pratt, J (2002) *Punishment and Civilisation*, London: Sage.

Prison Reform Trust/National AIDS Trust (2005) *Joint Report on the Spread of Contagious Diseases in Prison*, London: PRT/NAT.

Radzinowicz, L (1968) *Report of the Advisory Committee on the Penal System on the Regime for Long-term Prisoners in Conditions of Maximum Security*, London: HMSO (the 'Radzinowicz Report').

Radzinowicz, L and Hood, R (1986) *A History of English Criminal Law, Vol 5: The Emergence of Penal Policy*, London: Stevens.

Ramsbotham, D (2003) *Prisongate*, London: Free Press.

Rawlings, P (1999) *Crime and Power*, London: Longman.

Raynor, P and Vanstone, M (2002) *Understanding Community Penalties*, Milton Keynes: Open University Press.

Reiman, J (2007) *The Rich Get Richer and the Poor Get Prison: Ideology, Class, and Criminal Justice*, 7th edn, Boston, MA: Allyn and Bacon.

Rickford, D and Edgar, K (2005) *Troubled Inside: Responding to the Mental Health Needs of Men in Prison*, London: Prison Reform Trust.

Rodley, N (1999) *The Treatment of Prisoners under International Law*, 2nd edn, Oxford: Clarendon Press.

Rothman, DJ (1971) *The Discovery of the Asylum*, Boston, MA: Little, Brown and Co.

Ruggiero, V, Ryan, M and Sim, J (eds) (1996) *Western European Penal Systems: A Critical Anatomy*, London: Sage.

Rusche, G (1933) 'Labour market and penal sanction: thoughts on the sociology of criminal justice', in D Melossi (ed) (1998) *Sociology of Punishment*, Aldershot: Ashgate, pp. 69–96.

Rusche, G and Kirchheimer, O (1939; 2003) *Punishment and Social Structure*, London: Transaction.

Rutherford, A (1984) *Prisons and the Process of Justice: The Reductionist Challenge*, London: Heinemann.

Rutherford, A (1993) *Criminal Justice and the Pursuit of Decency*, Oxford: Oxford University Press.

Ryan, M (2005) *Penal Policy and Political Culture*, Winchester: Waterside Press.

Ryan, M and Ward, T (1989) *Privatization and the Penal System*, Milton Keynes: Open University Press.

Scott, DG (2006) *Ghosts Beyond Our Realm: A Neo-Abolitionist Analysis of Prison Officer Occupational Culture and Prisoner Human Rights*, Unpublished PhD thesis, University of Central Lancashire.

Scott, DG (2007) 'The changing face of the English prison: a critical review of the aims of imprisonment', in Y Jewkes (ed) (2007) *Handbook on Prisons*, Cullompton: Willan Publishing, pp. 49–72.

Scott, DG and Codd, H (2008) *Controversial Issues In Prison*, Milton Keynes: Open University Press.

Scottish Prison Service (2006) *Annual Report and Accounts*, Edinburgh: SPS.

Scraton, P and Chadwick, K (1987) '"Speaking ill of the dead": institutionalised responses to deaths in custody', in P Scraton (ed) *Law, Order, and the Authoritarian State: Readings in Critical Criminology*, Milton Keynes: Open University Press, pp. 212–36.

Scraton, P, Sim, J and Skidmore, P (1991) *Prisons Under Protest*, Milton Keynes: Open University Press.

Scull, A (1977) *Decarceration: Community Treatment and the Deviant—A Radical View*, Englewood Cliffs, NJ: Prentice Hall.

Scull, A (1979) *Museums of Madness*, Basingstoke: Palgrave Macmillan.

Scull, A and Andrews, J (2001) *Undertaker of the Mind: John Monro and Mad-Doctoring in Eighteenth-Century England*, Berkeley, CA: University of California.

Seddon, T (1996) 'Drug control in prisons', *Howard Journal*, 35(4), pp. 327–35.

Sellin, JT (1976) *Slavery and the Penal System*, New York: Elsevier.

Sim, J (1990) *Medical Power in Prisons: The Prison Medical Service in England, 1774–1989 (Crime, Justice and Social Policy)*, Milton Keynes: Open University Press.

Sim, J (1994) 'Reforming the penal wasteland? A critical review of the Wolf Report', in E Player and M Jenkins (eds) *Prisons After Woolf: Reform Through Riot*, London: Routledge, pp. 31–45.

Sim, J (2008) *The Carceral State: Power and Punishment in a Hard Land*, London: Sage.

Simon, J (2007) *Governing Through Crime: How the War on Crime Transformed American Democracy and Created a Culture of Fear*, New York: Oxford University Press.

Sivanandan, A (2001) 'Poverty is the new Black', *Race and Class*, 43(2), pp. 1–6.

Social Exclusion Unit (2002) *Reducing Reoffending by Ex-Prisoners*, London: HMSO.

Solzhenitsyn, AI (1963) *One Day in the Life of Ivan Denisovich*, Harmondsworth: Penguin.

Sparks, R, Bottoms, AE and Hay, W(1996) *Prisons and the Problem of Order*, Oxford: Clarendon Press.

Spierenburg, P (1984) *The Spectacle of Suffering*, Cambridge: Cambridge University Press.

Stern, V (1989) *Imprisoned by Our Prisons: A Programme for Reform*, London: Unwin Hyman.

Straw, J (1997) *Prison Reform Trust Lecture 1997*, London: Prison Reform Trust.

Sykes, G (1958) *Society of Captives: A Study of a Maximum Security Prison*, Princeton, NJ: Princeton University Press.

Taylor, AJP (1968) 'Introduction', *The Communist Manifesto*, Harmondsworth: Penguin.

Thomas, JE (1972) *The Prison Office*, London: Routledge Kegan Paul.

Toch, H (1975) *Men in Crisis: Human Breakdown in Prison*, Chicago, IL: Aldine.

Toch, H (1977) *Living in Prison: The Ecology of Survival*, New York: Free Press.

Tomlinson, M (1996) 'Imprisoning Ireland', in V Ruggiero, M Ryan and J Sim (eds) *Western European Penal Systems: A Critical Anatomy*, London: Sage, pp. 194–227.

Vagg, J (1994) *Prison Systems: A Comparative Study of Accountability in England, France, Germany and The Netherlands*, Oxford: Clarendon Press.

Van Swaaningen, R (1986) 'What is abolitionism?', in H Bianchi and R van Swaaningen (eds) *Abolitionism: Towards a Non-Repressive Approach to Crime*, Amsterdam: Free University Press, pp. 9–21.

Van Swaaningen, R (1997) *Critical Criminology: Visions from Europe*, London: Sage.

Van Zyl Smit, D and Dunkel, F (eds) (2001) *Imprisonment Today and Tomorrow: International Perspectives on Prisoners' Rights and Prison Conditions*, 2nd edn, London: Kluwer Law International.

Von Hirsch, A (1976) *Doing Justice: The Choice of Punishment*, New York: Hill and Wang (Report of the Committee for the Study of Incarceration).

Wacquant, L (2008) *Deadly Symbiosis*, Cambridge: Polity Press.

Walliman, N (2006) *Sage Course Companion: Social Research Methods*, London: Sage.

Walmsley, R (2006) *World Prison Populations List*, London: International Centre for Prison Studies.

Webb, S and Webb, B (1922) *English Prisons Under Local Government*, London: Longman, Green and Co.

Weiss, R and South, N (eds) (1998) *Comparing Prison Systems: Toward a Comparative and International Penology*, Amsterdam: OPA.

West, DG and Farrington, DP (1973) *Who Becomes Delinquent?*, London: Heinemann.

Windlesham, L (2001) *Responses to Crime: Volume 4—Dispensing Justice*, Oxford: Clarendon Press.

Woodcock, J (1994) *Report of the Enquiry into the Escape of Six Prisoners from the Special Security Unit at Whitemoor Prison, Cambridgeshire, on Friday 9 September 1994*, London: HMSO (the 'Woodcock Report').

Woolf, LJ (1991) *Prison Disturbances April 1990: Report of an Inquiry, Part I*, London: HMSO.

Woolf, LJ (2002) 'Making punishments fit the needs of society', *Prison Service Journal*, (142), pp. 6–9.

Worrall, A and Hoy, C (2005) *Punishment in the Community*, Cullompton: Willan Publishing.

Wyner, R (2003) *From the Inside*, London: Aurum.

Young, J (1999) *The Exclusive Society: Social Exclusion, Crime and Difference in Late Modernity*, London: Sage.

List of cases

Becker v Home Office [1972] 2 QB 407, [1972] 2 All ER 676
Edwards v United Kingdom (2002) 35 EHRR 487
Ezeh and Connors v United Kingdom (2002) 35 EHRR 28
Hirst v United Kingdom (2004) 38 EHRR 40
Raymond v Honey [1983] 1 AC 1, [1982] 1 All ER 756
Stafford v United Kingdom, Application no. 46295/99 [2002] ECHR 2002-IV, 115

List of statutes

The following Acts of Parliament are listed in chronological order.
Transportation Act 1718
Hulk Act 1776
Penitentiary Act 1779
Act of Union 1800
(Scottish) Prison Act 1839
Prisons (Scotland) Administration Act 1860
Prison Act 1865
Prisons (Scotland) Act 1877
Probation of Offenders Act 1907
Criminal Justice Act 1948
Prison Act 1952
Prison Act (Northern Ireland) 1953
Criminal Justice Act 1982
Criminal Justice Act 1991
Human Rights Act 1998
Criminal Justice Act 2003

index

Tables are given in italics.